TURKEY'S DEMOCRACY UNDER CHALLENGE

HEARING

BEFORE THE

SUBCOMMITTEE ON EUROPE, EURASIA, AND EMERGING THREATS

OF THE

COMMITTEE ON FOREIGN AFFAIRS HOUSE OF REPRESENTATIVES

ONE HUNDRED FIFTEENTH CONGRESS

FIRST SESSION

———

APRIL 5, 2017

———

Serial No. 115–15

———

Printed for the use of the Committee on Foreign Affairs

Available via the World Wide Web: http://www.foreignaffairs.house.gov/ or
http://www.gpo.gov/fdsys/

———

U.S. GOVERNMENT PUBLISHING OFFICE

24–917PDF   WASHINGTON : 2017

For sale by the Superintendent of Documents, U.S. Government Publishing Office
Internet: bookstore.gpo.gov   Phone: toll free (866) 512–1800; DC area (202) 512–1800
Fax: (202) 512–2104   Mail: Stop IDCC, Washington, DC 20402–0001

COMMITTEE ON FOREIGN AFFAIRS

EDWARD R. ROYCE, California, *Chairman*

CHRISTOPHER H. SMITH, New Jersey
ILEANA ROS-LEHTINEN, Florida
DANA ROHRABACHER, California
STEVE CHABOT, Ohio
JOE WILSON, South Carolina
MICHAEL T. McCAUL, Texas
TED POE, Texas
DARRELL E. ISSA, California
TOM MARINO, Pennsylvania
JEFF DUNCAN, South Carolina
MO BROOKS, Alabama
PAUL COOK, California
SCOTT PERRY, Pennsylvania
RON DeSANTIS, Florida
MARK MEADOWS, North Carolina
TED S. YOHO, Florida
ADAM KINZINGER, Illinois
LEE M. ZELDIN, New York
DANIEL M. DONOVAN, JR., New York
F. JAMES SENSENBRENNER, JR.,
    Wisconsin
ANN WAGNER, Missouri
BRIAN J. MAST, Florida
FRANCIS ROONEY, Florida
BRIAN K. FITZPATRICK, Pennsylvania
THOMAS A. GARRETT, JR., Virginia

ELIOT L. ENGEL, New York
BRAD SHERMAN, California
GREGORY W. MEEKS, New York
ALBIO SIRES, New Jersey
GERALD E. CONNOLLY, Virginia
THEODORE E. DEUTCH, Florida
KAREN BASS, California
WILLIAM R. KEATING, Massachusetts
DAVID N. CICILLINE, Rhode Island
AMI BERA, California
LOIS FRANKEL, Florida
TULSI GABBARD, Hawaii
JOAQUIN CASTRO, Texas
ROBIN L. KELLY, Illinois
BRENDAN F. BOYLE, Pennsylvania
DINA TITUS, Nevada
NORMA J. TORRES, California
BRADLEY SCOTT SCHNEIDER, Illinois
THOMAS R. SUOZZI, New York
ADRIANO ESPAILLAT, New York
TED LIEU, California

AMY PORTER, *Chief of Staff*   THOMAS SHEEHY, *Staff Director*

JASON STEINBAUM, *Democratic Staff Director*

SUBCOMMITTEE ON EUROPE, EURASIA, AND EMERGING THREATS

DANA ROHRABACHER, California, *Chairman*

JOE WILSON, South Carolina
TED POE, Texas
TOM MARINO, Pennsylvania
JEFF DUNCAN, South Carolina
F. JAMES SENSENBRENNER, JR.,
    Wisconsin
FRANCIS ROONEY, Florida
BRIAN K. FITZPATRICK, Pennsylvania

GREGORY W. MEEKS, New York
BRAD SHERMAN, California
ALBIO SIRES, New Jersey
WILLIAM R. KEATING, Massachusetts
DAVID N. CICILLINE, Rhode Island
ROBIN L. KELLY, Illinois

CONTENTS

TURKEY'S DEMOCRACY UNDER CHALLENGE

WEDNESDAY, APRIL 5, 2017

House of Representatives,
Subcommittee on Europe, Eurasia, and Emerging Threats,
Committee on Foreign Affairs,
Washington, DC.

The subcommittee met, pursuant to notice, at 2:18 p.m., in room 2172, Rayburn House Office Building, Hon. Dana Rohrabacher (chairman of the subcommittee) presiding.

Mr. ROHRABACHER. Good afternoon. I call this hearing to order. Today, we return our attention to the political situation in Turkey. I could have waited 1 more minute. There you go. Okay.

Today, we return our attention to the political situation in Turkey. Those of you who have followed the work of this subcommittee will note that this is a topic we have dedicated significant time toward in the past. This has not been motivated by malice, but a sincere desire to keep the United States-Turkish relationship rooted firmly in shared interests and shared values.

As we meet now, voting is already under way in a referendum to rewrite the Turkish Constitution. Voting is expected to be completed later this month on April 16. If adopted, the new amendments to the Turkish Constitution will cement in law much of the power President Erdogan has already seized for himself. The new Constitution would see Turkey convert into a Presidential system, combining the head of state, head of government, and head of the ruling party all into a single powerful office.

Once all that is done, the Prime Minister's leading position will be eliminated. The President will be able to select his own Vice Presidents and his own Cabinet. The power of the legislature to check the executive branch would be drastically reduced.

After reviewing the proposed changes and the Council of Europe's Venice Commission, an advisory body of constitutional experts, concluded that these amendments that are being voted on by the Turkish people, "represent a dangerous step backwards," and that these changes put Turkey on a path towards, and I quote, "an authoritarian" regime.

This referendum is the latest in a long list of actions taken by the Turkish Government under Erdogan, and under Erdogan, we have seen, basically, the civil society, closed space for them; silencing the media; you have seen sidelining of the judiciary; and a neutering of the military, of course.

I recognize the traumatic and unsettling nature of the failed July coup, but Erdogan started down this path toward authoritarianism

(1)

long, long before that coup. President Erdogan's desire to maintain power at any cost is not good for the people of Turkey. It is not healthy for Turkey's democracy, obviously. It is not in the interest of Turkey. And Erdogan, if nothing else, is spoiling Turkey's relationship with Europe and the United States and, alarmingly, has opened up Turkey to a greater risk of attack by radical violent Islamists.

Lastly, while thousands of Turks have been unjustly fired and arrested, forced abroad, I need to highlight one particular case. And that is Reverend Andrew Brunson, an American citizen who has been needlessly detained in Turkey since last year. In February, I, along with 75 other Members of Congress, signed a letter to President Erdogan requesting his release. Sadly, Mr. Brunson remains in jail, and this case continues to be an impediment to our relationship.

I want to thank all of our members for coming today. I don't have many on my side of the aisle. I thank my Democratic colleagues for joining us today. I am going to yield to Mr. Meeks for his opening statement. Then each member will be granted 1 minute for an opening statement. And then we will hear from the witnesses.

Mr. Meeks.

Mr. MEEKS. Thank you, Chairman Rohrabacher, and for the opportunity to talk about the U.S.-Turkish relationship. I see we have got a full audience today, and the timing is interesting, as it is less than 2 weeks before the important constitutional referendum.

The timing is also unfortunate because I know how congressional hearings resonate in Turkey and are sometimes used to misrepresent the feelings of Congress. I do hope that this hearing helps foster better relations between our two countries and does not fuel anti-American sentiment in Turkey with either side.

Nevertheless, as someone who has visited Turkey several times and loved Turkey and particularly the Turkish people, it pains me to watch what is transpiring in that beautiful country. The attempted coup that we discussed in our last hearing in Turkey was a traumatic shock to the system. In the aftermath, President Erdogan sought to rid the government agencies of coup plotters, Gulenists and more, and what he has actually done is overreached, and he is not respecting due process or the basic tenets of democracy in what appears and is a power grab.

And I have already heard from several members of my community, in my constituency and folks from Queens, who are very concerned about the democracy and how it will continue in Turkey and whether or not those individuals who have been jailed and were not given due process, what will happen to them, and how long will this continue. This is of tremendous concern to me.

Now comes another test: The upcoming referendum that attempts to turn the Turkish Government into what is being called a Presidential system. The question is, why now? Is there a special need to formalize President Erdogan's power in light of threats that are real or imagined? Regardless of the outcome of the referendum, which seems to be hardly fair and free, I do not see how Turkish democracy wins.

In either scenario, the economy will continue to suffer; the brightest will continue to leave Turkey; and the space for a liberal

Turkey will become even smaller. And during this difficult time, our Secretary of State paid a visit without mentioning anything of the troubles I and our chairman have outlined.

It is difficult to speak honestly with allies in trouble. It is easier to skip that conversation and hide behind the rhetoric of the war against ISIS.

I hope that Mr. Flynn, Mr. Michael Flynn's role, who was a paid foreign agent in the Trump administration, has nothing to do with the egregious silence on the state of democracy in Turkey.

As I follow my former mayor's recent interest in Turkey, I hope that Mr. Giuliani's work to protect Turkish bankers does not seep into the Trump administration's position, for far too much is at stake.

We are discussing a NATO ally, and it is best for the United States that Turkey remain in NATO because a Turkey without that anchor is left in a difficult region and—it is an understatement—without support, without someone to work with them in the difficult nature of democracy. Both NATO and the U.S. have a tremendous opportunity and responsibility with our ally Turkey in this regard.

And despite the crackdown on freedom of speech in the Turkish press, despite the firing and jailing of tens, if not hundreds of thousands, of public servants, and despite the fact that this election will likely not be free and fair, people still in Turkey are in the streets demonstrating. The Turkish people are resisting and persisting in the face of great odds.

This is the hope that I want to keep alive. The Turkish people care about their democracy. All you have to do is ask them, and that is why they are in NATO, and that is why I am here today to listen and to learn from our witnesses. And I would like to thank Ms. Durakoglu for being here with us again. I know she was up on the Hill and the State Department for a while, and I just wanted to say I am happy to see you back here on the Hill.

I yield back.

Mr. ROHRABACHER. All right. Mr. Sherman.

Mr. SHERMAN. A couple of notes.

Mr. ROHRABACHER. 1 minute.

Mr. SHERMAN. A couple of notes on history.

Early in the 20th century, the Armenian people were subject to a genocide that will be recognized here in this building today. And Turkey would be a better ally of the United States if we had a government that came to terms with its history rather than one that tried to engage in genocide denial.

Early in the 21st century, Erdogan welcomed, or at least turned a blind eye, to ISIS fighters going across Turkey, using Turkey as a place for R&R and recuperation and medical training, in part because they were fighting against Assad. Now, he faces a blowback from the same ISIS fighters that he once welcomed or at least gave safe passage to.

Erdogan is not a democratic leader. He is, as others have pointed out, moving Turkey toward authoritarianism. That being said, there is an effort to designate the Muslim Brotherhood as a terrorist organization. I for one would want to make sure that any such action did not include the AKP, which may have some philo-

4

sophical roots with the Brotherhood but is not, at least at this stage, a terrorist organization.

I yield back.

Mr. ROHRABACHER. Mr. Sires.

Mr. SIRES. Thank you, Mr. Chairman, for holding today's hearing to evaluate the challenges facing democracy in Turkey, and thank you to our panelists for being here today.

While Turkey has been a strategic partner of the U.S. and a key NATO ally in a volatile region, I am deeply troubled by the actions of President Erdogan and his government following last year's coup and the implications these actions have on the future of democracy in Turkey.

Amid the atmosphere of distrust, Turkey's government has detained or dismissed thousands—tens of thousands—of personnel within its military, judiciary, and civil service, and the education system, as well as taken over or closed various businesses, schools, and media outlets. It is unclear how long this type of purge will last, but it is imperative that the U.S. and our European partners continue to press Turkey to follow the rule of law.

The emerging relationship between Erdogan and Putin also contributes to not only the uncertain future of U.S.-Turkey relations but to the future of democracy in Turkey as well. In less than 2 weeks, we will have a clearer picture of the trajectory of democracy in Turkey when Erdogan's proposed constitutional changes to increasingly consolidate his power will be put to a vote.

Hopefully, the referendum will be held freely and fairly without undue influence. The Turkish Government should take the opportunity to, in these unstable times, to unite Turkey and not to intensify division and mistrust. I look forward to hearing from our esteemed panel of witnesses on their views of the current events and the impact on the U.S.-Turkey relationship, and thank you.

Mr. ROHRABACHER. All right. Thank you very much.

Mr. Cicilline.

Mr. CICILLINE. Thank you, Chairman Rohrabacher, and Ranking Member Meeks for calling this important and timely hearing.

Turkey remains a key ally in the fight against ISIS yet has had considerable challenges of its own in recent years. President Erdogan has consolidated power in recent years, culminating with the planned referendum this month that would give him sweeping authority and jeopardize the Turkish democratic system moving forward.

I am greatly concerned by Erdogan's government's use of mass arrests of civil servants, critics, journalists, academics, and anyone he perceives as an opponent. The government's use of a state of emergency to carry out a sweeping crackdown against anyone who dissents with his views is counter to democratic values.

The Trump administration has thus far shown no willingness to criticize the undemocratic and repressive tendencies of the Erdogan government, a position which I fear will only lead to further bad and destabilizing behavior. Moreover, 100 years after the fact, the Turkish Government continues to deny its well-established role in the Armenian genocide and continues to target Armenian, Kurdish, and other minorities within its borders.

5

As we approach the commemoration of the 102nd anniversary of the Armenian genocide, it is my hope that this is the year in which the American President will fully recognize the atrocities perpetuated against the Armenian people by the Ottoman Empire beginning in 1915.

The Armenian people deserve full recognition and acceptance of their suffering. I look forward to today's testimony and to having an opportunity to discuss these issues in more detail.

And I thank you and yield back.

Mr. ROHRABACHER. Thank you.

And Ms. Kelly.

Ms. KELLY. I pass.

Mr. ROHRABACHER. All right.

Well, I would like to welcome our witnesses today, and I would ask if the witnesses could keep it down to 5 minutes and please submit anything more than that for the record, and that will be part of the record of this hearing.

I will introduce the witnesses, and then we will proceed down the line. First is David Phillips as director of the program on Peace-Building and Rights at Columbia University's Institute for the Study of Human Rights. He is also the author of a recently released book. There it is. I am a writer, and I always wanted to have a book, but I haven't got one yet. But thank you for sharing that with us today and the knowledge that you gained. Your book is entitled, "An Uncertain Ally," and it is specifically about Turkey. So we appreciate you sharing this expertise with us today as you did, sharing your talents, as a foreign affairs expert and senior advisor at the State Department.

We have with us also Mehmet Yuksel. I hope I am pronouncing this correctly.

Mr. YUKSEL. Mehmet Yuksel.

Mr. ROHRABACHER. Yuksel, okay, why don't you pronounce it for us?

Mr. YUKSEL. Yuksel.

Mr. ROHRABACHER. Yuksel. Okay. He is a representative of the People's Democratic Party, or the HDP, in the United States. He has spent his career working in the United States and in Europe to promote conflict resolution between Turks and the Kurdish minority. We appreciate you being with us today and sharing your insights.

And Ali Cinar is President of the Turkish Heritage Organization and has a long track record in terms of working on U.S.-Turkey bilateral relations. He has been both a journalist and a businessman and is well versed on the issues that we are going to be discussing today.

And I am going to ask Naz to pronounce her last name for us again.

Ms. DURAKOGLU. Durakoglu.

Mr. ROHRABACHER. Okay. I am going to get it. All right. You got it. If anybody can pronounce Rohrabacher correctly, I am going to give them an award as well. She is a senior fellow at the Atlantic Council's Digital Forensic Research Lab. She comes to us having recently left the State Department. I remember her having here on several occasions. She was a senior advisor on Europe and Eurasia topics, and before that, she worked on Capitol Hill, including as a minority staff director for this subcommittee.

So welcome back, and we appreciate all of our witnesses.

We would start off with Mr. Phillips and then just say 5 minutes, and we will just go right down the line, and at that point, we will up for dialogue between the members and the witnesses.

So Mr. Phillips.

STATEMENT OF MR. DAVID L. PHILLIPS, DIRECTOR, PROGRAM ON PEACE-BUILDING AND RIGHTS, INSTITUTE FOR THE STUDY OF HUMAN RIGHTS, COLUMBIA UNIVERSITY

Mr. PHILLIPS. Thank you, Mr. Chairman. I would like to address two falsehoods that define the U.S.-Turkey relationship. The first is that Turkey is a secular democracy. It is neither secular nor is it a democracy.

In 1998, Mr. Erdogan read a poem, "The mosques are our barracks, the domes are helmets, the minarets our bayonets, and the faithful are soldiers." He was convicted to a 10-month prison term for inciting hatred based on religious differences.

The other myth is that Turkey is an important member of NATO. That may have been the case, but given the close collusion between Turkey and jihadists, including the Islamic State, beginning in 2013, there is serious cause for concern. NATO is more than a security partnership. It is a coalition of countries with shared values. Because Turkey today, under Erdogan, is Islamist, antidemocratic, and hostile to human rights, if NATO were being established, Turkey simply wouldn't qualify as a member.

On the subject of Islamism, when the AKP won a resounding electoral victory in July 2007, instead of addressing human rights concerns or the Kurdish question, Erdogan introduced legislation to permit the wearing of a hijab in public institutions. Just 2 weeks ago, women were allowed to wear the hijab in the military.

There is widespread corruption in Turkey. On December 17 of 2013, Mr. Erdogan was recorded speaking to his son about how to dispose of tens of millions of dollars of assets, including plans to buy luxury apartments on the Bosporus. There have been 50,000 WikiLeaks recordings of his son-in-law, Berat, colluding with ISIS to sell oil from Syria, the proceeds of which, at its peak, was generating $3 million a day and was used to support the Islamic State.

Serious concerns exist about freedom of expression and assembly. The 1991 law on the fight against terrorism is used to silence critics. Article 8 of the Anti-Terror Act applies selectively to restrict freedom of expression. Article 301 of the penal code makes it a crime to denigrate Turkishness.

When Turks gathered in Gezi Park in May 2013 to protest plans to build a shopping mall in a green space, they were violently dispersed by riot police. Protests spread to 60 cities as a result of police brutality. There was scant media coverage of the events while they were going on. Turkish national television broadcast a documentary about the migration of penguins.

Provocateurs were tracked after Gezi, and they were rounded up. The national intelligence agency is allowed to gather personal data without court order. By November 2016, Turkey has more journalists in jail than any country in the world. In fact, a third of all journalists that are jailed come from Turkey. There are about 150 imprisoned. About 160 media outlets have been closed.

On the transparency report of Twitter censorship, Turkey ranks high for crackdown on social media. It was reported in the Turkish media that President Erdogan called imprisoned journalists terrorists, child molesters, and murderers.

Gag orders have been issued for specific activities, including reporting on the transfer of weapons from Turkey to Islamic State fighters. The editor in chief of Cumhuriyet was sentenced to 5 years for reporting weapons transfers to Syria. There is some contestation about Turkey's collusion with ISIS. We have conducted an extensive research report, which I have submitted to the committee for the record.

Let's remember that Fethullah Gulen and Tayyip Erdogan were fast friends and partners. Their relationship soured and Gulen was accused of running a parallel state, of orchestrating the corruption crackdown in 2013. After the coup of July 15, 2016, there was a systematic crackdown that you have referenced. About 140,000 Turks have either been imprisoned or removed from their positions. These include members of the security as well as educators.

Turkey has become an outlier in Europe. The European Parliament voted to suspend Turkey's EU membership negotiations on November 24 of this year. When the Justice and Development Party wanted to send ministers to campaign for the referendum in Germany and in the Netherlands, they were not allowed to do so because of security concerns. Erdogan responded to that by calling Chancellor Merkel subject to Nazi measures. He described the Dutch action and Dutch Government as Nazi remnants and fascists. Recently a minister said that they would launch jihad in Europe if they were not allowed to campaign there, and they threatened to release 15,000 refugees a week into Europe if Europe and Turkey continued to head south in their relationship.

On minority rights, we will hear from Mr. Yuksel. Let me just say that there are serious concerns about Greek issues and Armenian issues. I chaired the Turkish Armenian Reconciliation Commission for 4 years. There was a legal opinion issued indicating that the events could be characterized as genocide. Recently, Turkey has intensified its repression against Armenians. It refused to submit the protocols on normalization for ratification. On Greek issues, the Ecumenical Patriarch still suffers great repression.

Mr. ROHRABACHER. Thank you very much.

Mr. PHILLIPS. In our discussion, I will discuss some recommendations with you.

[The prepared statement of Mr. Phillips follows:]

Testimony by:

DAVID L. PHILLIPS

Director of the Program on Peace-building and Rights
Columbia University's Institute for the Study of Human Rights

TURKEY'S DEMOCRACY UNDER CHALLENGE

U.S. House of Representatives
Committee on Foreign Affairs
Subcommittee on Europe, Eurasia, and Emerging Threats
Rayburn 2172

April 5, 2017

Introduction

Thank you, Mr. Chairman. I am pleased to participate in this Committee's hearing on challenges to democracy in Turkey.

There were early warning signs. In 1998, Tayyip Edogan made a public speech:

The mosques are our barracks, the domes our helmets, the minarets our bayonets, and the faithful our soldiers.

A court sentenced Erdogan to a ten-month prison term for "inciting hatred based on religious differences."

After the 2002 elections, Erdogan said: "Democracy is like a street car. You get off when you reach your destination."

When this committee held similar hearings last May, it was apparent that democracy was backsliding in Turkey. As I will report today, this trend has intensified. My analysis will address:

- Islamism;
- Corruption;
- Freedom of Expression and Assembly;
- Freedom of the Press;
- Terror Ties;
- Relations with the EU and NATO; and,
- Minority rights (Kurds, Armenians, and Greeks)

Turkey is called as a secular democracy. Turkey is neither secular nor a democracy. If the referendum passes on April 16, formalizing anti-democratic governance, the date will mark the death of Turkey's nascent democracy.

Turkey is heralded for its NATO membership. But NATO is more than a security alliance. It is a coalition of countries with shared values. Turkey under Tayyip Erdogan is an uncertain ally. Turkey is Islamist, anti-democratic, and a serial abuser of human rights. Turkey would not qualify as a member if NATO was established today.

Islamism

Mustafa Kemal Ataturk established the Republic of Turkey in 1923. He redefined the role of religion, strictly separating religion and government. Ataturk defined Turkey's republican identity through cultural values shared with Europe. Secularism gave primacy to reason over faith. It placed individualism over the divine.

After Ataturk, pious politicians increasingly challenged the country's secular elite. In response, the Constitutional Court banned Islamist parties. The military intervened in 1960, 1971, 1980, and 1997 to restore Kemalist order against leftist, conservative, and Islamist parties. In 1994, Erdogan was elected mayor of Istanbul. The Refah Party, with Erdogan in its leadership, was banned in 1997. Erdogan became prime minister when the AKP won national elections in 2002.

For Erdogan, human rights are Islamic rights. After emerging from prison in 1998, Erdogan found it expedient to espouse human rights in Western terms. Not because he believed in them, but because it advanced his political agenda to subordinate the security establishment under the guide of advancing Turkey's EU candidacy. Erdogan disassociated himself from political Islam, while embracing Islamic identity politics. For Erdogan, democracy and human rights were vehicles to advance Islamic expression.

Tensions between the AKP and the military escalated when Erdogan nominated Abdullah Gul to become president in 2007. Security officials were appalled that Gul, a devout Muslim, would occupy the office once held by Ataturk. To counter threats of a coup, Erdogan called early elections. On July 22, 2007, the AKP won 46.6 percent of the vote, which equated to 341 of the 550 seats in parliament. Erdogan used his political capital to push legislation allowing women to wear the hijab at universities and public institutions.

When the Turkish Supreme Court deemed the law unconstitutional, Erdogan threatened: "We are going to shut down the Constitutional Court." In 2008, the AKP sponsored a referendum on constitutional reform, giving the AKP-controlled parliament greater influence over the appointment of senior judges and prosecutors. Erdogan also intensified pressure on the military. Hundreds of retired military officers were arrested. Arrests were justified, citing a fantastic plot that included bombing mosques in Istanbul, staging the assault of a military museum by people disguised as religious extremists, and raising tensions with Greece by downing a Turkish plane over Greek air space. Turkey's army, navy and air force heads resigned to protest the arrests. Last month, a measure was adopted allowing females in the armed forces to wear the hijab while on duty.

Corruption

Single-party rule fostered a culture of corruption that touched the highest levels of government, as well as the Erdogan family. On December 17, 2013, police officers raided several homes, seized $17.5 million in cash, and detained fifty-two people with ties to the AKP. Prosecutors charged fourteen people with bribery, corruption, fraud, and money laundering. Four ministers resigned.

As the crackdown unfolded, Erdogan called Bilal, his son, instructing him to dispose of cash at several family homes. Wiretaps recorded the calls. At eight in the morning on December 17, 2013, Erdogan called Bilal: "Now I'm telling you, whatever you have in the house, get rid of it, OK?" Father and son spoke four times during the day. In their last conversation, Bilal indicated: [I still have] "30 million euros ($39 million) that we could not yet get rid of." Erdogan assured Bilal, "Whatever, we will deal with it." Bilal indicated "Berat Albayrak, (Erdogan's son-in-law and current minister of energy), "has an idea to buy villas from Sehrizar Apartments. What did you think?" The case was white washed. Prosecutors and police were fired and incriminating tapes destroyed to get rid of the evidence.

The case of Reza Zarrab warrants special mention. Zarrab, a dual Iranian-Turkish national was arrested by Turkish police in December 2013. Zarrab was charged with gold smuggling and bribing cabinet ministers. Erdogan made special efforts to shield Zarrab. He vouched for Zarrab's character, calling him a "philanthropist" whose work had "contributed to the country." Charges against Zarrab were dismissed, as a result of Erdogan's intervention.

When Iran was denied access to the SWIFT international money transfer system as a result of US sanctions, the Iranian government developed a strategy for by-passing SWIFT using Turkey's Halkbank. Zarrab sent money to front companies in China, identifying the transfers as export reimbursements. Funds were moved from the Chinese companies to companies in Turkey. The money was used to buy gold, which was transported to Iran via middlemen in Dubai. Selling Iranian gold and laundering the proceeds through Turkish banks violated US sanctions. On March 19, 2016, Zarrab was arrested at Miami International Airport.

Zarrab's indictment was unsealed in the Southern District of New York. Charges included defrauding the United States, money laundering, and violating the International Emergency Economic Powers Act, which regulates Iran sanctions. Kemal Kilicdaroglu, head of the People's Republican Party (CHP), predicted: "All the dirty laundry will come out. Many people won't sleep a wink tonight."

The probe is ongoing. Mehmet Hakan Atilla, Halkbank's vice president for international banking, was arrested in New York on March 27, accused of "a years-long scheme to violate American sanctions laws by helping Zarrab to use U.S. financial institutions to engage in prohibited financial transactions that illegally funneled millions of dollars to Iran."

The 2013 EU progress report highlighted corruption, expressing "concern" 39 times. According to the report, "The government's response to allegations of corruption targeting high-level personalities, including members of the government and their families, raised serious concerns over the independence of judiciary and the rule of law."

Freedom of Expression and Assembly

Turkey systematically denies freedom of expression and freedom of assembly. It uses the 1991 Law on the Fight against Terrorism to silence critics, alleging breaches of national security. Article 8 of the Anti-Terror Act is applied selectively to restrict freedom of expression. Article 301 of the Penal Code makes it a crime to denigrate "the Turkish Nation, the State of the Turkish Republic or the organs and institutions of the State." Article 216 of the Penal Code, which carries a mandatory prison term of up to three years, bans "incitement of hatred or violence based on ethnicity, class, or religion," targeting Kurds.

Turks resent Erdogan's authoritarianism and intrusion into their private lives. For example, Erdogan publicly called on women to bear at least three children. He made comments about their make-up, lipstick color, and what clothes women should wear. He recently called on Turks living in Europe to have five children in order to affect Europe's demography.

In May 2013, Turks protested plans for a shopping center in Gezi Park, camping in Gezi for 17 days. Though Article 34 of the constitution permits freedom of assembly, riot police attacked with tear gas and water cannons on May 30, 2013. While Gezi was the epicenter of protests, antigovernment demonstrations occurred in sixty cities across Turkey. Police brutality fueled civic unrest. There was scant media coverage of the Gezi protests. As the crackdown was unfolding, state media aired a documentary about penguins.

Gezi initiated a new phase in Turkey's crackdown on social media. Though Article 26 of Turkey's constitution guarantees freedom of expression and dissemination of thought, the government launched an investigation to track down tweets during the protest and expose "provocateurs." After Gezi, the government exercised increased powers to shut down websites. The Internet Law No. 5651 of February 2015 empowered Turkey's Telecommunication Directorate to block websites without court approval.

Adopted in April 2015, the Law Amending the Law on State Intelligence Services and the National Intelligence Organization allowed the National Intelligence Agency (MIT) to access personal data without a court order. It provided immunity to MIT personnel from legal violations committed in the course of their work. It also criminalized reporting on MIT's activities. A new law allowed sentences of up to nine years for publishing information from leaked intelligence material. Article 299 of the Penal Code established criminal liability for insulting the President. Between August 2014 and March 2016, the prosecutor opened 1,845 cases based on Article 299.

Press Freedom

By November 2016, Turkey had more journalists in jail than any country in the world. As many as 150 journalists, one-third of the total jailed worldwide, were imprisoned. More than 160 media outlets were closed by the end of 2016. The European Parliament (EP) issued its bi-yearly progress report on April 14, 2016. "Turkey still has one of the highest number of imprisoned journalists in the world." According to Freedom House, "Turkey does not have a free press." "Turkey remains top of Twitter's global censorship list," according to the latest Twitter Transparency report published on March 21." Erdogan called imprisoned journalists "terrorists, child molesters, and murderers (*Cumhurriyet*, 22 March 2017)."

Turkey uses a variety of techniques to suppress criticism. Journalists are prosecuted for terrorism, insulting public officials, or crimes against the state. Threats and physical attacks occur. Officials interfere with editorial independence and pressure media organizations to fire critical journalists. The government also exerts financial pressure. For example, the Dogan Group, which owns *Hurriyet* and *CNN Turk*, was penalized $3.2 billion in tax arrears.

Turkish courts and regulators issue gag orders on specific topics. A ban on allegations of MIT involvement in weapons shipments to Syria was imposed in February 2014. Another was issued in March 2014, restricting dissemination of leaked audio recordings of national security meetings. Can Dundar, editor in chief of *Cumhurriyet* was sentenced to five years for reporting on MIT's weapons transfers to ISIS in Syria.

Terror Ties

Turkey stepped up its supply of weapons to Islamist insurgents in Syria when the US failed to intervene after Syria used chemical weapons in August 2013. MIT established an infrastructure for supporting jihadists, ranging from weapons transfers to logistical support, financial assistance and medical services. Vice President Joe Biden confirmed Turkey's involvement (Harvard University, 2 October 2014). "Our allies in the region were our largest problem in Syria. The Turks...poured hundreds of millions of dollars and ten thousand tons of weapons into anyone who would fight against Assad." Biden continued, "President Erdogan told me, he's an old friend, 'You were right. We let too many people through.'"

Erdogan refuted Biden's claim. "My request from our friends in the United States is to make your assessment about Turkey by basing your information on objective sources." In response, Columbia University created an international research team based in the U.S. Europe, and Turkey. Columbia documented scores of credible reports on Turkey's cooperation with jihadi groups, including ISIS. (Copy attached)

Fethullah Gulen

Gulen and Erdogan were friends and partners. Hizmet ("Service"), a moderate Muslim network founded by Gulen, propelled the AKP's rise. Gulen provided resources and infrastructure to support the AKP and erode the secular bureaucracy. Gulen instructed his followers to infiltrate mainstream structures: "You must move within the arteries of the system, without noticing your existence, until you reach all the power centers." In 1999, Gulen was charged with undermining secularism and fled to Pennsylvania.

Erdogan blamed Gulen of running a "parallel state," with Gulenists permeating the judiciary, police, and the media. Erdogan accused Gulen of orchestrating the corruption crackdown in December 2013. Turkey is seeking his extradition for allegedly masterminding the failed coup of July 15, 2016.

Post-Coup Conditions

Erdogan warned his opponents, "They will pay a heavy price for this." He launched purges against oppositionists. *The New York Times* described the purges as a "counter-coup." Erdogan would "become more vengeful and obsessed with control than ever, exploiting the crisis not just to punish mutinous soldiers but to further quash whatever dissent is left in Turkey." A three-month state of emergency was declared, giving the government extraordinary powers, bypassing parliament and ruling by decree. The state of emergency was extended for a second three-month period, as the crackdown intensified. As of November 2016, more than 40,000 people had been arrested since the coup. More than 100,000 people were dismissed from state institutions including the judiciary, military, and security forces.

Roughly one-third of the 220 brigadier generals and 10 major generals were detained. One third of all admirals were arrested. Many majors and lieutenant colonels were taken into custody. About six thousand soldiers of various ranks, mostly conscript privates, were imprisoned and about nine thousand police officers dismissed. 262 Turkish diplomatic, military personnel have requested asylum in Germany

The education sector was decimated. About 21,000 teachers were suspended or fired. An additional 11,000 Kurdish educators were suspended for suspected links to the PKK. Every university dean in the country was forced to resign. Erdogan was given authority to appoint university heads.

The rule of law was undermined. 2,754 judges were dismissed, including members of the High Council of Judges and Prosecutors. A member of the Constitutional Court was arrested and charged with collusion. Ten members of Turkey's highest administrative court were detained. Under new state of emergency provisions, prosecutors were given permission to record lawyer-client conversations, and judges were empowered to deny the accused access to a lawyer for up to 3 months.

At least thirty governors were fired. The Ministry of Interior revoked the passports of 49,211 Turkish citizens. Private property was confiscated and retirement benefits canceled. The World Justice Index placed Turkey 99th out of 113 countries in its rule of law ranking, behind Iran and Myanmar.

Outlier in Europe

Turkey became a European Union (EU) candidate country at the EU Helsinki Summit in December 1999. EU candidate countries must meet economic and institutional requirements. They must also have "stable institutions guaranteeing democracy, the rule of law, human rights and respect for and protection of minorities." Actual negotiations would start when Turkey met the "Copenhagen criteria," which enshrine human rights.

The EP voted to suspend talks with Turkey on EU membership (24 November 2016), citing Erdogan's crackdown on political opponents after the failed coup. The resolution warned, "The government's actions are further diverting Turkey from its European path." The resolution passed overwhelmingly with 479 votes in favor, 37 against and 107 abstentions.

Erdogan doubled down by threatening to cancel the EU-Turkey deal on migrants. Tensions between Ankara and the EU worsened. When Germany refused to allow a campaign rally with Turkish ministers, citing security concerns, Erdogan accused the German government of "Nazi measures." When the Dutch government refused landing rights to Turkey's foreign minister for similar reasons, Erdogan described it as "Nazi remnants and fascists." On March 15, Turkey's Foreign Minister Mevlut Cavusoglu warned: "Holy wars will soon begin in Europe." That same day the interior minister threatened: "We could open the way for 15,000 refugees that we don't send each month."

Efforts to undermine democracy extend to countries in Europe as well as the United States. Revelations in Wikilinks document a systematic effort to camouflage Turkey's illicit lobbying efforts in the US. Payments to General William T. Flynn also represent influence peddling, including representation that violated the Foreign Agents Registration Act.

Minority Rights

EU Membership requires the protection and promotion of minority rights in accordance with international standards. Turkey is not in compliance when it comes to Kurdish, Armenian and Greek issues.

Kurdish Issues

The AKP's sweeping victory in 2007 resulted from inroads with Kurdish voters. The AKP appealed to Kurds through its conservatism and by expanding social services, building roads, schools and hospitals in predominantly Kurdish areas of the Southeast. Erdogan publicly acknowledged the Kurdish issue, promising an end to civil war. Kurds were tired of conflict. They hoped that the AKP would pursue a peace process with the PKK, resulting in disarmament and demobilization. Kurds also hoped that the AKP would amend the constitution, recognizing Kurdish identity. These hopes were misplaced.

In January 2016, more than 1,400 Turkish academics signed a "peace petition" calling for an end to Turkey's "deliberate massacre and deportation of Kurdish people." The petition, entitled "We will not be party to this crime", also called for peace talks with the PKK. The government responded with a broadside on academic freedom and freedom of expression. Erdogan said, "We are not in the position to seek permission from the so-called academics. These [people] should know their place." Erdogan referred to the peace petition as a "betrayal." He called its signatories "darkest of the dark" and "a fifth column" for terrorists. According to Erdogan, "They commit the same crime as those who carry out massacres."

The 2016 EP report deplored "the increasingly authoritarian tendencies of the Turkish leadership." It expressed concern about "rapidly deteriorating" security situation in the country, especially in the Southeast. The report insisted that, "All operations by security forces must be proportional and not take the form of collective punishment." According to the EP, "The Turkish government has a responsibility to protect all people living on its territory, irrespective of their cultural or religious origins."

The AKP received 40.9 percent of the vote on June 7, 2016. The tally was less than Erdogan expected. The vote was the first time in four general elections that support for Erdogan decreased. The progressive and pro-Kurdish Democratic People's Party (HDP) crossed the 10 percent barrier with 13.1 percent, which equated to 80 seats in the parliament. Erdogan blocked the formation of a coalition government, resulting in early elections. In July, Erdogan cynically re-started Turkey's civil war with the PKK in a play for nationalist voters. He promised stability and the return of economic growth. Fear mongering worked. On November 1, Erdogan tightened his grip on power, establishing single party government with nearly 50 percent of the vote. The tally was a big step towards realizing Erdogan's goal of constitutional reform and an executive presidency, pending parliamentary approval and a popular referendum, which is scheduled for April 16, 2017.

Eliminating the HDP as an effective opposition, the Turkish government jailed 13 HDP members of parliament on terrorism charges and took direct control of 82 municipalities in the Southeast, incarcerating elected mayors. Thousands of other members of the Kurdistan Communities Union

(KCK) were arrested. According to the HDP, 5,471 HDP party officials, including heads of provincial and district branches, were detained since the coup. The arrests undermined the HDP's ability to conduct a campaign over the upcoming referendum.

A report of the Office of the United Nations High Commissioner for Human Rights (March 2017) documented security operations in a number of Southeast provinces affecting civilians. Between July 2015 and December 2016, about 2,000 people were killed. The report documented numerous cases of excessive use of force; killings; enforced disappearances; torture; destruction of housing and cultural heritage; incitement to hatred; prevention of access to emergency medical care, food, water and livelihoods; violence against women; and severe curtailment of the right to freedom of opinion and expression as well as political participation. The most serious human rights violations reportedly occurred during periods of curfew, when entire residential areas were cut off. Movement was restricted around-the-clock for several days at a time. Half a dozen cities were attacked. Cizre's destruction rivals the destruction of Aleppo in Syria.

Armenian Issues

From 2001 to 2004, I chaired the Turkish Armenian Reconciliation Commission (TARC), whose work represented enormous progress addressing the Armenian Genocide. TARC facilitated participation of both sides in a legal opinion recognizing that the UN definition of genocide fit the Armenian experience. TARC also facilitated the agreement of joint recommendations to concerned governments on how to establish and improve relations. Contact between Turkish and Armenian civil society developed rapidly and continues to show progress. As President Reagan recognized in 1981, Armenians suffered the first genocide of the 20th Century with over 1.5 million victims; Armenian Genocide Remembrance Day is April 24.

In 2009, the Armenian and Turkish governments signed protocols on how to advance their relationship by establishing diplomatic relations, lifting the Turkish blockade of Armenia, and dealing openly with unresolved problems. Armenian President Serge Sarkisian stood by those agreements. However, Erdogan reneged refusing to submit the protocols to parliament for ratification. His anti-Christian and anti-Armenian rhetoric appeals to the Turkish nationalist base and exacerbates racism.

The Erdogan government is currently seeking to control the election of a new Armenian Church Patriarch in Istanbul. It has reversed prior trends toward objective education on the millennia old Armenian history in Turkey. Where the Armenian Church used to own over 5,000 churches and religious institutions, today it is allowed less than fifty. During more positive times and with assistance from the courageous mayor of Diyarbikir, Armenians were allowed to renovate and reopen the historic Saint Giragos Church. Under the pretext of the war on terror, however, the Turkish government expropriated the Church falsely claiming it wanted to repair damage. Local residents believe the government plans to replace destroyed minority neighborhoods with high-end condominiums. Better-off Syrian refugees could be resettled there. Turkey has also played an unhelpful role in US and international efforts to resolve peacefully the Nagorno-Karabakh conflict.

Greek Issues

Ecumenical Patriarch Bartholomew, the spiritual leader of the second largest Christian Church in the world with 300 million followers, resides in Istanbul. The Ecumenical Patriarch's religious freedom is severely curtailed in Turkey. By refusing to recognize his "legal identity" as the Ecumenical Patriarch, the government of Turkey justifies the confiscation of thousands of Ecumenical Patriarchal properties including monasteries, church buildings, an orphanage, private homes, apartment buildings, schools and land. Turkey began returning some of those properties a few years ago, but then stopped.

The Ecumenical Patriarch's seminary at Halki, which had operated since 1844, was forced to close in 1971. The Government of Turkey has inserted itself into the Church's selection of future Ecumenical Patriarchs, suggesting it may again insist on the right to veto Ecumenical Patriarchs elected by the Church's Holy Synod.

Turkey's recent treatment of Hagia Sophia in Istanbul is cause for concern. Hagia Sophia is a UNESCO World Heritage Site, built in 537 and maintained as the world's largest Christian cathedral for nearly 1,000 years. Muslims then utilized the structure as a mosque for almost 500 years. In 1935, it was opened as a museum for all faiths. Just last year, for the first time in 85 years the Qur'an was recited at Hagia Sophia. Other steps are anticipated, converting Hagia Sophia into a mosque.

The Constitutional Referendum

Parliament authorized constitutional amendments on January 20, 2017. A referendum to approve 18 amendments to the constitution will be held on April 16, 2017. If approved, the referendum will establish an executive presidency. It will eliminate checks and balances. The current parliamentary system will be canceled, and the Office of the Prime Minister abolished. The president would appoint and dismiss ministers. The number of seats in parliament will be increased to 600 from 550. Changes brought about by adoption of the referendum will limit the power of parliament to impeach the president. Changes will also be made to the Supreme Board of Judges and Prosecutors, undermining judicial independence. The referendum will destroy Turkey's prospect of gaining membership in the EU. By abandoning its Western orientation, the referendum will change the way Turkey is governed, establishing one-man rule and transforming Turkey into a dictatorship.

Free and Fair?

Erdogan has tried for years to consolidate his power by establishing an executive presidency. He has used his current executive powers to enhance the "yes" vote. The AKP's control of media has hampered the "no" campaign. The state of emergency declared after the coup created an environment hindering efforts of the "no" campaign. Erdogan intimidated opponents by accusing them of supporting the coup plotters. Opponents of the referendum have suffered coercion, harassment, and arrest. The American pastor Andrew Brunson was jailed. Incarcerating HDP deputies and lifting their parliamentary immunity undermined the coalition of opponents. The HDP has filed an application at the European Court of Human Rights regarding continued arrest of its co-leaders, Selahattin Demirtas and Figen Yuksekdag. The police limited the activities of "no" campaigners. Local government officials denied "no" campaigners permission to hold rallies and limited their access to public facilities. The CHP released a report identifying 78 measures Erdogan used to suppress support for the "no" campaign (1 March 2017). The CHP intends to challenge the parliamentary vote at the Constitutional Court, citing irregularities and intimidation of deputies. For example, a CHP member with an artificial arm and leg was attacked on the floor of the parliament and her prosthetics ripped from her body.

Turkey's descent to dictatorship is occurring in plain sight. US officials must not turn a blind eye. They should see Turkey as it is, not how it used to be, or how they wish it were.

Recommendations

- Review Turkey's NATO membership. There are extensive political criteria for joining NATO. But no one ever thought a NATO member would go rogue, requiring expulsion. The North Atlantic Council could establish a "Compliance Review Committee," using a scorecard to grade the democracy and human rights performance of Member States. If a country, such as Turkey or Hungary, receives a failing score for consecutive years, its NATO membership would be temporarily suspended.

- Diversify air combat operations, mitigating threats by Turkey to block US access to Incirlik Air Force. Alternatives include British bases in Cyprus – Akrotiri and Dhekelia, as well as bases in Jordan, Kuwait, and Iraqi Kurdistan.

- Develop a dossier of war crimes committed by Turkish security against the Kurds, and support a commission of inquiry. The risk of Interpol red bulletins freezing the assets and restricting travel of Erdogan, members of his inner circle, and family members could have a positive influence on Turkey's behavior.

- Have additional hearings of the House Committee on Foreign Affairs. Consider the referendum, including whether votes were accurately counted, as well as the conditions in which the referendum was conducted. Members of Congress should support initiatives to directly assist democratic forces and civil society in Turkey.

- Continue to prosecute with appropriate zeal the case of Reza Zarrab. In 2016, federal prosecutors successfully defeated Zarrab motions for bail and dismissal. Trial is now set for August. It should proceed apace.

- Resist politicization of Gulen's extradition review. The US Justice Department must decide if Turkish evidence is strong enough to merit extradition, and if Gulen could receive a fair trial in Turkey in the context of post-coup conditions. The State Department has an important role to play in extraditions. But extradition is fundamentally a legal, rather than a political, determination, as established in the US-Turkey Extradition Treaty.

Mr. ROHRABACHER. All right. Thank you.
Mr. Yuksel.

STATEMENT OF MR. MEHMET YUKSEL, REPRESENTATIVE TO THE UNITED STATES, PEOPLE'S DEMOCRATIC PARTY IN TURKEY

Mr. YUKSEL. Dear Honorable Chairman Dana Rohrabacher and distinguished members of the House subcommittee. It is an honor for me to testify today on crucial development in Turkey.

I would like to discuss a few major threats to democracy in Turkey and the rule of law.

The constitutional amendments that are proposed by President Erdogan and AK Party project an authoritarian system of governance whereby absolute power is held by a single person. Even though the proposed constitutional amendments have not been legally accepted, the amendments have been implemented and practiced under the state's rule of emergency.

Let me list the several indication for extralegal and single-person rule in the Kurdish area especially and against the Kurdish political parties.

Since the failed coup attempt, July 2016, 11 HDP deputies have been arrested and jailed, including co-chair Selahattin Demirtas and Figen Yuksekdag. The freedom of speech that democracy supports and Turkey's Constitution guarantees is the basic allegation that co-chair Demirtas for what he is subjected to over 500 years of detention.

Between July 2015 and March 2017, 8,930 HDP members were detained and 2,782 party members have been imprisoned; 494 HDP offices have been attacked, burned down, and vandalized, including HDP headquarters. Rallies were attacked and law enforcement support for these attacks has been widely documented.

Around 10,000 municipality and humanitarian employees of Kurdish origin have been suspended from their positions. The government has also confiscated the monetary assets of the people they remove from their positions. Almost all of the media outlets protesting in Kurdish, both local and national levels, were closed. Kurdish journalists are arrested and sent to the prison. Even daycares where Kurdish is spoken have been shut down by the government.

In the prisons, especially, the torture and ill-treatment methods have mainly been widely practiced, and there is ongoing hunger strike in the prisons for 50 days in some of the prisons.

The number of internally displaced in southeastern Turkey is estimated between—estimated about half a million people, mainly the citizens of origin Kurdish. The humanitarian aid to the IDP is very limited. All of the local humanitarian NGOs have been shut down.

The governmental aid to IDPs is also conditioned upon leaving their properties and lands, which will bring a demographical change in the Kurdish-populated areas. Many people have already left the areas.

The authorities have also imposed extended around-the-clock curfews on 30 towns and neighborhoods, prohibiting any movement without permission for extended periods of time, lasting up to several months. These months-long around-the-clock curfews have prevented civilians to evacuate the towns where the Turkish military conducted the operation.

The lack of emergency services to the sick and wounded ultimately contribute to a high toll of deaths in these operations. In total, 2,000 people were killed during these operations and under the curfew.

The public prosecutors have consistently refused to open an investigation on the reported killings. Failure to conduct the investigation of the killings is clear violation of constitutional and international human rights laws.

In Cizre, 189 me, women, children were trapped in the basements of the buildings that were heavily shelled by Turkish security forces. These people did not have any access to water, food, and medical attention. Even though the trapped were calling for attention and help from the international community via phone conversations and videos, they were burned alive by the Turkish security forces.

The Kurdish cities, which has been attacked by the security forces is Silvan—Sur, Silvan, Lice, Nusaybin, Dargecit, Cizre, Silopi, Sirnak, Idil, and Yuksekova. Those towns have been destroyed by the Turkish security forces. The images of the destroyed Kurdish cities resemble Syria's civil war images, which you have also a copy of the photo of some destructions.

On March 10, 2017, the United Nations Human Rights office published a report detailing massive destruction, killings, and numerous of other serious human rights violation committed by Turkish forces between July 2015 and December 2016 in Turkey.

Honorable chairman and distinguished members of the House subcommittee, my people in Turkey are going through a full-scale assault, which could be viewed as a form of genocide. The Turkish authorities have seen the Kurdish identity as the main enemy. Fighting this enemy, they have been conducting a slow-motion genocide.

I urge the United States House of Representatives to authorize this concern, to launch an investigation on crimes against humanity committed in southeastern Turkey and the Kurdistan of Turkey; to take action to put further pressure on Turkish authorities to respect democracy, rule of law, and human rights; ensure the freedom of speech with releasing thousands of political prisoners and journalists.

I also urge the House of Representatives committee to act upon mediating peace talks and negotiation in Turkey to achieve a peaceful political solution to the Kurdish issue in Turkey and to encourage Turkish authorities to resume peace talks and mediate the peace process and achieve a political solution.

With the approaching referendum on the constitutional amendments, Turkish society has become further polarized across different social and ethnic and sectarian groups. What has been quite worrisome is the fact that the ruling AK Party has been arming its supporters, and state authorities have been encouraging attacks on dissident groups within the country.

If the situation in Turkey is not taken seriously and the democracy and the rule of law——

[The prepared statement of Mr. Yuksel follows:]

MEHMET YUKSEL

THE REPRESENTATIVE TO THE UNITED STATES
OFFICE

PEOPLE'S DEMOCRATIC PARTY (HDP) IN TURKEY.

HOUSE COMMITTEE ON FOREIGN AFFAIRS,
SUBCOMMITTEE ON EUROPE, EURASIA, AND
EMERGING THREATS

HEARING: "TURKEY'S DEMOCRACY UNDER
CHALLENGE"

APRIL 5, 2017

Dear Honorable Chairman Dana Rohrabacher and distinguished members of the House Subcommittee,

It is an honor for me to testify today on a crucial development in Turkey. I would like to discuss a few major threats to democracy and rule of law in Turkey.

The constitutional amendments that are proposed by President Recep Tayyip Erdogan and the ruling AK Party projects an authoritarian system of governance, whereby absolute power is held by a single person.

Even though the proposed constitutional amendments have not been legally accepted, the amendments have been implemented and practiced under the State of Emergency Rule.

Let me enlist several indications of this extralegal, single-person rule:

Since the failed coup attempt in July 2016, the immunity of 55 out of 59 HDP law makers has been removed. Following this, 11 HDP deputies have been arrested, including the Co-Chair Selahattin Demirtas and Co-Chair Figen Yüksekdag. The freedom of speech that democracy supports and Turkey's Constitution guarantees is the basic allegation against Co-Chair Demirtas for what he is subjected to over 500 years of detention.

Between July 22, 2015, and March, 27 2017, 8,930 HDP members were detained; and
2782 party members have been imprisoned. 494 HDP offices have been attacked; burned or vandalized, including the party headquarters. HDP rallies were attacked and law enforcement's support for these attacks have been widely documented, even on social media.

At the 84 municipalities run by the pro-Kurdish Democratic Regions Party (DBP), 88 co-mayors and 6 deputy co-mayors were dismissed and replaced by state appointed trustees. The mayors and co-mayors are currently under arrest. These mayors and co-mayors were all democratically elected by the people with overwhelming majority.

Around 10,000 municipality and humanitarian employees of Kurdish origin have been suspended from their positions. The government has also been confiscating the monetary assets of people they remove from their positions.

Almost all of the media outlets broadcasting in Kurdish at both local and national levels were closed. Kurdish journalists are arrested and sent to prisons. Even daycares where Kurdish is spoken have been shut down by the government.

Speaking of prisons, the torture and ill-treatment methods, namely beating and punching of detainees; sexual violence including rape and threat of rape; deprivation of basic needs, such as water, food and sleep; deprivation of medication and treatment; forcing detainees to kneel handcuffed from behind for hours; verbal abuse, psychological violence, and intimidation have been prevailing in Turkish prisons.

These methods of torture and ill-treatment recently led to a large-scale hunger strike among prisoners. The HDP Co-Chair Selahattin Demirtas has also joined the hunger strike to raise the awareness for torture.

The number of Internally displaced persons (IDPs) in South-East Turkey is estimated between 355,000 to half a million people, mainly citizens of Kurdish origin. The humanitarian aid to the IDPs is very limited. All of the local humanitarian NGOs have been shut down. The government aid to IDPs is also conditioned upon leaving their properties and land, which would bring a demographical change in the Kurdish-populated areas. Many people have already left their homes.

Since the failed coup attempt in July 2015, the Turkish government forces have been conducting security operations in a number of South-Eastern provinces, involving thousands of troops serving with combat-ready infantry, artillery and armoured army divisions, as well as the Turkish Air Force. The authorities also imposed extended around-the-clock curfews on over 30 towns and neighborhoods prohibiting any movement without permission for extended period of time, lasting up to several months. These months-long around-the-clock curfews have prevented civilians to evacuate the towns where the Turkish military conducted operations. The lack of emergency services to the sick and wounded ultimately contributed to the high death toll of operations. In total of 2,000 people were killed during those operations and curfews. The public prosecutors have consistently refused opening investigations on the reported killings. Failure to conduct investigations on the killings is a clear violation of constitutional and international human rights law obligations.

In the coldest months of the year, the late January and early February of 2016, for weeks, in the town of Cizre, 189 men, women and children were trapped in basements of the buildings that were heavily shelled by the Turkish security forces. These people did not have access to water, food and medical attention. Even though the trapped were calling for attention and help from the international community via phone conversations and videos, they were burned alive by the Turkish security forces.

The Kurdish provinces and cities that Turkish security forces targeted includes Sur, Silvan, and Lice in the province of Diyarbakir, Nusaybin, and Dargecit in the province of Mardin, Cizre, Silopi, Idil, Sirnak city center in the province of Sirnak, and Yuksekova in the province of Hakkari. These towns have been destroyed by the Turkish security forces.

The images of the destroyed Kurdish cities resemble the Syrian civil war images.

The scale of the unnecessary destructions, including damages to properties and businesses, in Kurdish cities and towns is estimated around 21 billion US dollars.

On March 10, 2017 the UN human rights office published a report detailing massive destruction, killings and numerous other serious human rights violations committed by Turkish forces between July 2015 and December 2016 in southeast Turkey[1].

According to Human Rights Association, the Turkish government has conditioned financial compensation for destroyed housing upon the signature of declaration by owners that their property was destroyed by "terrorist activities". Families who have been forced to sign such declaration have reported this practice as an effort to falsify the historical

---

[1] http://www.un.org/apps/news/story.asp?NewsID=56330

record of the 2015-16 events and an effort to bring impunity to the state officers committed to human rights violations. It has also been reported that a number of families, who had been compelled to abandon their destroyed homes during the period of the security operations, were also forced to sign away the ownership of their properties.

Honorable Chairman Dana Rohrabacher and the Distinguished members of the House Subcommittee,

My people in Turkey are going through a full-scaled assault, which could be viewed as a form of genocide. The Turkish authorities have seen the Kurdish identity as the main enemy. Fighting this enemy, they have been conducting a slow-motion genocide. In fact, when we look at the eight stages of genocide published by Genocide Watch, we see that the Turkish government is indeed committing genocide against a minority.

On November 18 2016, the United Nations Special Rapporteur on the promotion and protection of the right to freedom of opinion and expression, expressed grave concerns about the "draconian" measures being used to erode independent opinion and expression in Turkey.

I urge the United States House of Representatives to address these concerns; to launch investigations on the crimes against humanity committed in South-East Turkey. I urge the United States House of Representatives to take action to put further pressure on the Turkish authorities to respect democracy, rule of law and human rights, and ensure the freedom of speech with releasing thousands of political prisoners and journalists. I also urge the House of Representatives to act upon mediating peace talks and negotiations in Turkey and achieve a peaceful and political solution in Turkey to the Kurdish issue with encouraging the Turkish authorities to resume the peace talks and mediate the peace process to achieve a political solution.

With the approaching referendum on the constitutional amendments, Turkish society has become further polarized, across different social, ethnic, and sectarian groups. What has been quite worrisome is the fact that the ruling AK Party has been arming its supporters and state authorities have been encouraging attacks on the dissident groups within the country. If the situation in Turkey is not taken seriously and democracy and the rule of law in Turkey are not restored and rescued immediately, the country would face a large-scale civil war. Unfortunately, Turkey slowly but steadily is moving into chaos that leads to destabilizing the region further, in which we, the Kurds and other minorities would pay the heaviest price.

———————

Mr. ROHRABACHER. Thank you very much.
Mr. Cinar.

STATEMENT OF MR. ALI CINAR, PRESIDENT, TURKISH HERITAGE ORGANIZATION

Mr. CINAR. Good afternoon, Chairman, Ranking Member, and members of the subcommittee. It is an honor for me to testify today.

I am sure everyone would agree that 2016 was a particularly challenging year for Turkey and U.S. relations. There are disagreements and tensions over two major security issues, U.S. support of the PYD in Syria and Turkey's request for the extradition of Fethullah Gulen.

Understanding Turkey's democracy that is under challenge requires a comprehensive review of its domestic and regional risks. Terrorism continues to be the Turkey's number one security concern.

Overall, more than 270 people lost their lives in at least 12 major terror attacks by ISIS and PKK in Turkey, making 2016 a year of terror.

July 15 coup attempt, which was carried out by a faction with the Turkish armed forces, took a considerable toll on the Turkish nation. According to the Turkish Government, the coup attempt was organized by Fethullah Gulen and his followers. The Majority of Turkish people, including opponents of President Erdogan, believe that Gulen was the organizer of the coup attempt.

Gulen's network's influence of state institutions in Turkey was a well-known fact. For the first time in its history, Turkey, a country that is all too familiar with the periodic military disruptions, was able to stop a military coup, but it claimed 249 lives and injured over 2,000 people.

Turkey had survived an enormous threat and had to make difficult choices in the aftermath of the coup attempt. The emergency rule, which is still in effect, was aimed at taking the necessary measures and eliminating the complex national security risks that it created.

Turkey is gearing up for a historical referendum on April 16 when voters will decide whether or not to approve constitutional amendments that will shift Turkey's current parliamentary system to an executive Presidency. Upcoming referendum is an attempt by the Turks to start a new chapter, a chapter that doesn't involve any military imposed constitution.

Under the proposed changes to the Constitution, the President will be elected directly by the people with more than 50 percent of the votes, which means that there will be a better representation of the national will. The Turkish Parliament will remain involved in the political process and able to investigate the President, if needed.

Considering the challenges Turkey faces, my understanding is that the proposed changes will set the foundation for a more stable and secure Turkey. Don't we, the United States, need a much stronger ally in the region?

The Kurdish issue. Since 1980, Turkey has been experiencing a violent conflict with the Kurdistan Workers' Party. PKK is classified as a terrorist organization by United States, NATO, and European Union. The fight between the PKK and the Turkish state cost more than 40,000 lives.

When looking at the Kurdish issue in Turkey today, it is important to separate Turkey's Kurdish population from the PKK terrorist group. There are concerns about certain HDP members maintaining links to PKK or otherwise supporting the terrorist group, such as in case of some HDP members attending the funerals of PKK terrorists, meeting at their base camp in Kandil, and posing photos. It must also be remembered that, despite a base that is broadly Kurdish, the HDP is not de facto representative of all Kurds in Turkey.

Freedom of expression and the media constitute an important pillar of human rights in Turkey. It is a fundamental freedom guaranteed under the Constitution and other relevant legislation. It is important to note that the post-coup-attempt state of emergency has required extraordinary actions in order to ensure the stability and security of Turkey. Those journalists who have been detained or arrested under the state of emergency have been charged with serious crimes, which include spreading propaganda for terrorist organizations such as PKK and FETO.

Domestic remedies exist for those who believe they have been wrongfully suspected in antiterrorism investigations. The Inquiry Commission on the State of Emergency Measures addresses the applications from citizens who feel they have been wrongfully persecuted. This provides an effective domestic legal remedy to any false accusations.

U.S.-Turkey relations are more important now than ever. Turkey and Turkish democracy is experiencing an exceptional period of stress due to the security concerns. A weaker destabilized Turkey will be a disaster not just for citizens of Turkey but for Europe, NATO, and U.S. As Joint Chiefs Chairman General Dunford said during an Ankara visit, an express willingness to work through these issues and share perspectives will mean stability in the region.

The U.S. remains the ideal example of such democracy, and it is important now more than ever that Washington and Ankara maintain and improve their strategic and historic relationship in order to ensure the security of both their countries.

I would like to thank you again, Mr. Chairman and the committee members, for giving me the opportunity to be a part of this hearing today.

[The prepared statement of Mr. Cinar follows:]

TESTIMONY OF ALI CINAR, PRESIDENT OF TURKISH HERITAGE
ORGANIZATION
HOUSE COMMITTEE ON FOREIGN AFFAIRS, SUBCOMMITTEE ON
EUROPE, EURASIA, AND EMERGING THREATS HEARING: TURKEY'S
DEMOCRACY UNDER CHALLENGE APRIL 5, 2017

Chairman Rohrabacher, Ranking Member Meeks, Members of the
Subcommittee:

It is an honor for me to testify before you today. As a first generation
American, I have had the privilage to take important leadership roles
with two of the oldest Turkish-American umbrella organization –
Assembly of Turkish American Associations (ATAA) in Washington,
DC and Federation of Turkish-American Associations (FTAA) in New
York City. As the President of Turkish Heritage Organization, I
continue to dedicate myself to advance U.S. – Turkey relations. I am
very much aware about the importance of these hearings and I feel
particularly privilaged to be invited to this hearing room again for a
witness.

I think "Turkey's Democracy Under Challenge " is a suitable title for
this hearing. Regardless of where one stands on his/her views on
Turkey, I am sure everyone would agree that 2016 was a particularly
challenging year for Turkey and U.S. – Turkey relations. Exceptional
security challenges, including an attempted coup on July 15 and an
increase in deadly terror attacks carried out by groups like Daesh, the
PKK, and TAK have compounded U.S.-Turkey relations, which have
suffered a series of setbacks regarding disagreements and tensions
over two major security issues: U.S. support of the YPG in Syria and
Turkey's request for the extradition of Fethullah Gulen.

Understanding Turkey's democracy that is under challenge requires a thorough review of its domestic and regional risks. Terrorism continues to be Turkey's number one security concern. Escalation of the conflict between the Kurdistan Workers Party (PKK) and the Turkish state in 2016, ignited a wave of deadly terror attacks carried out by the Kurdistan Freedom Hawks (TAK) in cities like Istanbul, Ankara, and Kayseri. The renewal of this conflict is compounded by the increasing threat posed by Daesh, which successfully carried out a series of large-scale attacks in Turkey. These attacks made it clear that Turkey was facing an unprecedented security threat emanating from Syria that needed to be addressed. Overall, more than 270 people lost their lives in at least 12 major terror attacks in Turkey, making 2016 a year of terror.

The July 15 Coup Attempt, which was carried out by a faction within the Turkish Armed Forces (TSK), took a considerable toll on the Turkish nation. According to the Turkish government, the coup attempt was organized by U.S.-based Turkish exile Fethullah Gulen and a group of his followers that the Turkish government has labeled the Fethullah Gulen Terror Organization (FETO). Turkey's 26th Chief of the General Staff, Gen. (Ret.) M Ilker Basbug, who was jailed following the Ergenekon Trials, delivered a special address in Washington, D.C. as Turkish Heritage Organization's guest. Gen. Basbug told the audience he had no doubt that the coup attempt was organized by followers of Fethullah Gulen.

Similarly, Lt. Gen. Ismail Hakki Pekin, the former head of Turkey's military intelligence; Colonel Judge Ahmet Zeki Ucok, former military judge who has conducted investigations into the infiltration into the Turkish Armed Forces of followers of Pennsylvania-based Turkish cleric Fethullah Gulen; and Nedim Sener, who has investigated the role of Gulen-affiliated security forces in the assassination of Turkish-Armenian journalist Hrant Dink, spoke about the dangerous nature of the Gulen network when they visited Washington, D.C. as Turkish Heritage Organization's guests.

Following the coup attempt, the Turkish government formally requested Gulen's extradition to Turkey and presented the U.S. government with evidence showing Gulen's involvement in multiple crimes in Turkey. The extradition is one of the major areas of concern for Turkey with regard to its relations with the U.S.

It may be difficult to grasp the dangerous nature and capabilities of the Gulen movement for those who are not familiar with it but Turks and Americans from Turkish heritage are well aware of this organization's history and extensive world-wide network. Gulen network's infiltration of state institutions in Turkey was a well known fact. However, at the time both the Turkish and U.S. governments turned a blind eye to the organization "when it suited them."

Colonel Judge Ucok, who helped conduct military investigations into the Gulen network's infiltration during his tenure at the Air Force Attorney General's office, claimed that investigations had shown evidence that during the period between 1986 and 2006, 30,000 officers could have been connected to the Gulen movement. He estimated that during the following decade, an additional 40,000 could have entered into the armed services, thus making the number of affiliated officers approximately 100,000 by the present day. He said that of the 358 generals in the Turkish Armed Forces, 160 had been connected to this organization.

For the first time in its history, the Republic of Turkey, a country that is all too familiar with periodic military interferences, was able to stop a military coup but it claimed 248 lives and injured over 2000 people. Regardless of what we think about Turkey's democracy, the truth is that this coup attempt was going to undermine Turkey's democratic institutions, political parties and many other rights and liberties – exacerbating the existing domestic and regional risks and possibliy initiating a civil war.

Republic of Turkey had survived an enourmous threat and had to make difficult choices in the aftermath of the coup attempt. The emergency rule, which is still in effect, was aimed at taking the necessary precautions and eliminating the complex national security risks that it posed. According to Turkish newspapers, more than 113 thousand people were arrasted for charges related to FETO. Close to 42 thousand people were released following the appropriate investigations.

As it entered its sixth year, the civil war in Syria became Turkey's biggest regional security risk in 2016. Turkey has continued to be a reliable and effective partner in the fight against Daesh. After opening up Incirlik Air Base in July 2015 for use by the Global Coalition to Counter ISIL as part of Operation Inherent Resolve, Turkey launched its own operation in August 2016 in northern Syria to counter Daesh as well as the People's Protection Units (YPG), which Ankara views as a terrorist organization due to its links to the PKK.

With Operation Euphrates Shield in northern Syria, Turkey declared that it was exercising its right to self-defense (codified under Article 51 of the UN Charter) and officially became the first anti-Daesh coalition country to use ground forces in Syria.6 However, continued U.S. support of the YPG — which Washington considers an effective partner in the fight against Daesh — has aggravated and severely antagonized Turkey's threat perceptions during a period in which Turkey is suffering from attacks by both Daesh and Kurdish nationalist terror groups.

Operation Euphrates Shield holds considerable significance for Turkey. Following the coup attempt in July, there were both domestic and international concerns about the state of the TSK and about Turkey's institutional strength as a critical NATO member. In addition to addressing border security concerns and confronting terror groups,

Operation Euphrates Shield provided Turkey the opportunity to re-affirm its military strength and capability not only to its allies but also to its adversaries.

The ongoing civil war in Syria and the fight against Daesh continue to pose significant risks not only for Turkey but also for its allies. The Syrian conflict has exposed Turkey's domestic and regional vulnerabilities and undermined its security. It has strained U.S.-Turkey relations, which worsened even further after the coup attempt. Various disagreements between Turkey and the U.S. – especially over Syria drove Turkey closer to Russia. As a result, near the end of 2016, Moscow and Ankara worked closely together to negotiate a humanitarian ceasefire in Aleppo that would pave the way to a 2017 international meeting on a Syrian settlement in Astana, Kazakhstan. Although the rapprochement between Russia and Turkey has distanced the U.S. from this process, Ankara has expressed its willingness to improve its relations with Washington under the new presidential administration in the U.S.

In additon to significant security risks, the ongoing civil war in Syria also poses a significant humanitarian aid concerns for Turkey. While EU was seeking ways to stem the flow of refugees, both the Turkish government and NGOs have expended ample time and resources to support the 3 million refugees in Turkey with little assistance from the international community. Turkey remains at the forefront of global humanitarian aid efforts, ranking second on the 2016 Global Humanitarian Assistance report's list of top global donors. Even though Turkey is the largest refugee hosting country in the world, it is only the 10th highest recipient of aid. There is a major need for more aid to support large refugee populations in host countries such as Turkey.

The observations that I make in Turkey as well as in Washington clearly indicate that continuation of complications between Washington and Ankara – will not only severely damage bilateral defense cooperation between the two largest militaries in NATO but will also contribute to the destabilization of both Turkey and its region.

All of these challenges and enormous risks should be taken into consideration when evaluating Turkey's domestic and foreign policy motives. Turkey's domestic security will continue to be vulnerable to the conflict in Syria, and for that reason, Ankara cannot adequately address the threats it faces from myriad terror groups without strong cooperation with the U.S. on Syria.

Turkey is gearing up for a historical referendum on April 16, when voters will decide whether or not to approve constitutional amendments that will shift Turkey's current parliamentary system to an executive presidency. The idea of executive presidency is not new in Turkey. Former Presidents Turgut Ozal, Suleyman Demirel have introduced it but they were unable to pursue it due to the political conditions at the time. As someone who lived through the 1980's military coup d'etat and the constitution that was established afterwards in 1982, it is important to emphasize that Turkey is not a "classical" parliamentary system. In fact the existing constitution was set up to address the expectatios of military for a president that would come from a military background. In other words, the existing constituion is geared more toward protecting the Turkish state from the people than guaranteeing political and civil rights. From this perspective, the proposed changes to Turkey's constitution should be seen as a natural urge.

Turkey may not be a perfect democracy but one has to recognize that despite numerous challenges and setbacks, politial and civil rights has significantly improved since the 1980's. The upcoming referendum is an attempt by the Turks to start a new chapter – a chapter that does not involve any military imposed constitution. Political stability, something that is difficult to grasp for under the military imposed constitution will be the ultimate goal of this referandum.

I am not an expert on constitutinal law and government. However, it is important to analyze the root causues and needs behind the proposed changes. Turkey traditionally had been governed by a bureaucratic-military secular elite. Up until recently, Turkish military remained as the invisible hand that monitored and threatened the political establishment. In 2007, military blocked then AK Party Foreign Minister Abdullah Gul's run for the presidency – a complete disregard to politial process. This is just one example at the highest level. Turkey and Turks have been living under this invisible hand for over 35 years now!

Turkey and Turks hope that the proposed changes will finaly change this three decades-long influence and interference that has negatively impacted the natural course of democratic progress. Under the proposed changes to the constitution, the President will be elected directly by the people with more than 50% of the votes, which means that there will be a better representation of the national will. Additionally, current issues with jurisdiction of the President is extraordinarily large. The new system proposes greater responsibility and accountability as well as faster and more efficient decision making process. Administrative obstacles and red-tape, which have severe consequences on Turkey's overall governance, will be eliminated. Not to mention that the proposed system will create a strong barrier against coups.

The Current Version: Judicial power shall be exercised by *independent courts* on behalf of the Turkish Nation.**The Proposed Version:** The Current Version: Judicial power shall be exercised by *independent and impartial courts* on behalf of the Turkish Nation. **Why:** This would increase confidence into the Judiciary. FETO like illegal structures will not be able to infiltrate to the Judiciary.

Who has the Power? The Grand National Assembly can take the decision to send the president to the Supreme Court with two-thirds of its members secret votes.

Judicary in the new Proposed Presidential System: The Council of Judges and Prosecutors shall be composed of **13** regular members; and shall comprise **two chambers**. The Council's *four members* are appointed from among judges and prosecutors by the **president**. *Seven members* are appointed by the **Grand National Assembly**. The minister of justice is the head of the council and the undersecretary is its natural member.Democratic legitimacy would be consolidated. Factionalism would come to an end. Example: **The Netherlands:** All members **appointed by the King** upon the proposal of the Justice Minister. **Spain:** All members **appointed by the King** upon the proposal of the Parliament. **Norway:** 9 members. **2 appointed by the Parliament**. The **King appoints 7** upon the proposal of the Government.

I wanted to give some examples of the proposed Presendential system. The Turkish Parliament will remain to ve active and involve with the execution and able to investigate the President if needed.

The most important part is to have a A stronger system will increase the country's influence in the region and across the world.

Don't we-U.S – need a much stronger NATO Ally in the Region?

I would like to make some highlights on Turkey's Current Issues and Future of Partnership w U.S especially after April 16th:

We will learn the results on April 16th but no matter what happens US-Turkey partnership will remain stronger despite some disagreements.

Security:
- Especially PYD&PKK and FETO are the two top major issues for the relationship. Many members of congress don't believe that FETO was behind the coup attempt but many evidences show that FETO was

behind of the coup. PYD and FETO are the big terror threats for Turkey along w ISIS.

While Turkey considers the PKK/PYD to be a terrorist group affiliated to the PKK, which has waged war against Turkey since 1984, the U.S. sees the PKK/PYD as its ground ally against Daesh in Syria. Turkey launched Operation Euphrates Shield on Aug. 24 and completed mission last week. As a result: the operation was ensure the security of turkey, purge isis terrorities from turkish borders, to eliminate operational force of the terror PKK-PYD and ISIS to ensure stability securyithof region. More than 2500 ISIS terrorist were neutrailized more than 600 terrorist captured- more than 71 Turkis Military staff martred . Life in the purges areas went back to normal and thousands of syrians went back their homelands

Turkey is ready to support for fighting against ISIS in the region but concern remains on the US support to PYD. Several NGPs including Amnesty IntHuman Rights Watch and Syrian Network forhuman Rights report continuous human right violoations and ethnic leasing campaign conducted bt PYD-YPG.

Turkey has all the capabilities and ready to cooperate w US on ground fight against DAESH

-FETO: Turkey would like Fettullah Gulen to be extradited ASAP. If U.S believes Turkey as a strong ally on this case, U.S should take a look evidences more seriously and Turkey needs to be more patient on the U.S justice system.

Since we talk about the respect of the countries justice system, **The** extradition treaty signed by U.S-Turkey in 1979 - **treaty's 10th article says that in cases of urgency, if Turkey or the U.S. suspects anyone, the host country needs to arrest the suspect for 60 days until documents for extradition are submitted to the executive authority of the requested party.**

The "Kurdish Issue"

The "Kurdish issue" in Turkey is so-named because previous governments in Turkey restricted the rights and representation of ethnic Kurds, and this situation was exacerbated by violence against citizens of Turkey in the name of Kurdish separatism.

Since 1980, Turkey has been experiencing a violent conflict with the Kurdistan Workers' Party (PKK). The PKK is classified as a terrorist organization by Turkey, the U.S., and the EU. The fight between the PKK and the Turkish state has cost more than 40,000 lives.

In the 2000s, the AKP-led Turkish government initiated a "Kurdish opening" in an effort to find a political solution to this decades-long conflict. This opening included pursuing reforms that would allow for greater cultural rights. As one example of progress, in recent years, several Kurdish-language television and radio stations have been established in Turkey and courses teaching the Kurdish language and dialects have been created. This is a far cry from the days when Kurdish was banned in various forms under previous governments.

As part of this "Kurdish opening," the Turkish government pursued a peace process with the PKK aimed at ending the violence of the previous decades. This process collapsed in 2015.

When looking at the "Kurdish issue" in Turkey today, it is important to disassociate Turkey's Kurdish population from the PKK terrorist group.

The only "issue" the government of Turkey has is with PKK terrorists and their affiliates, who attack and kill citizens of Turkey of all backgrounds. It is important to note that the resurgence of the PKK conflict in Turkey is directly tied to the ongoing conflicts in Syria and Iraq. The chaos on Turkey's borders has strengthened the PKK by allowing it to continue operating from northern Iraq while strengthening its affiliates in Syria.

There are significant links between the PKK and the Democratic Union Party (PYD) and its armed wing, the People's Protection Units (YPG), in northern Syria. In addition to sharing an ideology and a devotion to Abdullah Ocalan, both the PKK and the PYD/YPG also share fighters, who may be fighting with the PKK one week and with the YPG the next.

The PYD-led cantons in northern Syria have also served as a training ground for terrorists who go on to conduct attacks in Turkey, as was the case of Seher Cagla Demir, who killed 37 people in a bombing in the heart of Ankara in March 2016.

In the West, there is a narrative that YPG and PKK advances against ISIS are victories for human rights. Juxtaposed against ISIS, many militant and terrorist groups look tame. But the need to defeat ISIS does not erase the fact that both the YPG and the PKK are terrorist organizations. The latter in particular has the blood of thousands of Kurds and Turks on its hands in Turkey alone.

Turkey has also been a victim of ISIS. In 2016, ISIS killed more than 100 people in Turkey – including foreigners. For Turkey, both ISIS and the PKK pose significant, deadly threats. A whitewashing of groups like the YPG and the PKK only serves to elongate conflicts in Syria, Iraq, and Turkey.

It is paramount for Turkey and the PKK to return to a peace process that will enable this conflict to be resolved once and for all. For this to happen, the U.S. needs to stand behind its NATO ally and help create the conditions for peace. This includes heeding Turkish concerns about U.S. support for the YPG while also working with

Turkey and other regional actors to negotiate an end to the Syria conflict. As long as there is a war on Turkey's borders, there will be the threat of spillover into Turkey's domestic issues.

The recent detentions and arrests of a number of MPs from the People's Democratic Party (HDP) must be understood in the context of the PKK conflict. Last May, immunity from criminal prosecution was lifted from over 100 members of the Turkish parliament, including MPs from every political party represented in parliament. Following this move, all affected members except some HDP MPs gave depositions regarding ongoing investigations into potential criminal activities. Turkish courts issued warrants for the HDP MPs in order to secure depositions. Since then, some have been remanded into custody while others have been released.

The HDP is a political party that passed the election threshold to enter the Turkish parliament, and it should continue to be included in the Turkish parliament as such. As a party with a broad Kurdish base, it will likely play an essential role in any new peace process between the Turkish state and the PKK, as it did in the past. Nevertheless, there are concerns about certain HDP members maintaining links to the PKK or otherwise supporting the terrorist group, such as in the case of some HDP members attending the funerals of PKK terrorists. These concerns need to be addressed. It must also be remembered that despite a base that is broadly Kurdish, the HDP is not the de facto representative of all Kurds in Turkey.

Freedom of Expression and the Media

Freedom of expression and the media constitute an important pillar of human rights in Turkey. It is a fundamental freedom guaranteed under the Constitution and other relevant legislation.

This does not mean, however, that mistakes have not been made in the past regarding ensuring this fundamental right. The abuses and fabrications of the Ergenekon and Sledgehammer trials, which were carried out by corrupt officials tied to FETO, are just one example.

Today, media in Turkey includes a diverse and wide variety of domestic and foreign print, television, radio, and online news outlets. In Turkey, there are over 7,000 newspapers and journals as well as more than 200 TV stations and more than 1,000 radio stations that reach national and local audiences. Each regularly exercises free speech without intervention from the government.

There are 110,000 Associations and 50,000 foundations currently operating in Turkey. In recent years, Turkey has undertaken a series of comprehensive judicial reforms in line with both international and EU standards and principles for the protection and promotion of freedom of expression and the media.

There is no Turkish legislation that includes any provision that would lead to imprisonment of journalists on account of their journalistic work. Everyone is equal before the law without any distinction as to his or her profession.

It is important to note that the post-coup-attempt state of emergency has necessitated extraordinary actions in order to ensure the stability and security of Turkey. Those journalists who have been detained or arrested under the state of emergency have been charged with serious crimes, which include spreading propaganda for terrorist organizations such as FETO and the PKK. Turkey has suffered repeated attacks and loss of life from both of these groups, and it is necessary to take actions that prevent further violence, including by pursuing criminal investigations against those who support these organizations.

Domestic remedies exist for those who believe they have been wrongfully suspected in the anti-terrorism probes. The Inquiry Commission on the State of Emergency Measures addresses applications from citizens who feel they have been wrongly persecuted. This provides an effective domestic legal remedy to any false accusations.

U.S.-Turkey Relations More Important Now Than Ever

Today, Turkey is beset by three major terrorist groups – the PKK, ISIS, and FETO. Violent conflicts in Syria and Iraq have direct ramifications for Turkey's own security. Turkey – and Turkish democracy – is experiencing an exceptional period of stress due to these security concerns.

Many of the actions taken under the current state of emergency have been pursued in order to return Turkey to a state of security and stability.

However, the Turkish government must also be cognizant of how these actions are carried out.

There are concerns that many innocents have been caught up in the Turkish government's efforts to extract members of FETO and other terrorist groups from the ranks of the military, police, judiciary, and academia.

It is imperative that the government continue to pursue programs like the Inquiry Commission on the State of Emergency Measures to give legal recourse to citizens who have been negatively affected.

Already, 31,000 individuals have been reinstated in their jobs after having been removed under the state of emergency measures, and 300 institutions that were previously closed under the state of emergency have been reopened.

While trials and detentions continue, it is essential that the Turkish government works to ensure fair and speedy trials and to prevent undue suffering while individuals remain in custody. Allegations of abuse of prisoners must be addressed when and where they are made.

A strong and stable Turkey will be a more beneficial partner for the U.S. It is important, then, for the U.S. to understand the exceptional situation Turkey is now in and to support its partner in its pursuit of stability.

As Turkey reconciles with the events of July 15 and their aftermath while also defending itself against spillover from the conflicts in Syria and Iraq, it is more important than ever for the U.S. and Turkey to maintain an open dialogue. Officials in both Washington and Ankara, need to return to a tenor of solidarity, respect, and shared commitment toward the realization of each country's interests.

As a NATO ally with the second largest military in the alliance, Turkey is a crucial security partner for the U.S. A weaker, destabilized Turkey will be a catastrophe not just for citizens of Turkey but for Europe, NATO, and the U.S. It is important for both Washington and Ankara to be able to engage in honest but respectful discussions with each other even in the face of disagreements or concerns. As General Joseph Dunford said on a November 2016 visit to Turkey, "an express willingness to work through these issues and share perspectives will mean stability in the region."

The July 15 coup attempt shook Turkey to its core and called into question its democratic resilience. However, the incredibly courageous response shown by the Turkish public as the coup attempt was unfolding made one thing clear: the Turkish people want a strong, free, and fair democracy.

The U.S. remains the preeminent example of such a democracy, and it is more important now than ever that Washington and Ankara maintain their strategic and historic relationship in order to ensure the security of both of their countries.

I would like to thank you again Mr. Chairman and Committee Members for giving me the opportunity to be a part of this hearing today.

Mr. ROHRABACHER. Thank you very much.

And we wanted to make sure that we had somewhat of a balance to this hearing, and that is always important to have at least one point of view that differs.

And we thank you for coming today. And knowing that that is a challenge in today's society, to step forward with your testimony, we appreciate it very much.

You may proceed.

STATEMENT OF MS. NAZ DURAKOGLU, STRATEGIST AND SENIOR FELLOW, DIGITAL FORENSIC RESEARCH LAB, ATLANTIC COUNCIL

Ms. DURAKOGLU. Thank you, Chairman Rohrabacher, Ranking Member Meeks, and members of the committee. It is an honor to testify before you both as a witness and a former staffer on this committee under Congressman Bill Keating.

Congressman Bill Keating's commitment to public service and my work with all of you continues to be an inspiration to me.

The Turkish referendum on April 16 should not be viewed as a standalone domestic event; rather, a critical moment in Turkey's history with wider implications for the transatlantic community and NATO alliance.

The vote comes at a time of heightened fear, polarization, and trauma for Turks, who have endured one of the deadliest years in their recent history, a failed coup on July 15, and a subsequent purge of institutions across Turkey.

This environment colors the constitutional package at the center of the referendum. If passed, Turkey's parliamentary structure would change into a Presidential system with few checks and balances. I detail these changes in my written testimony but would like to emphasize that under the proposed constitution, the new President would exercise almost complete executive control with the ability to appoint and dismiss all ministers with no legislative buy-in.

Further, the proposed amendments weaken instead of strengthen the Turkish judiciary and give the President the power to appoint two-thirds of the country's senior judges. No matter the outcome, Turkey's partners must prepare to engage with the Turkish state that is in battle for its future.

The four key areas to watch are transatlantic security, energy cooperation, economic prosperity, and democratic values. Having the second largest military in the NATO alliance, Turkey has a profound influence on international security matters. The use of Turkey's Incirlik Air Base allows for 25 percent more strikes against ISIS in Syria, and much of the United States' humanitarian aid work there is based out of Turkey.

Last week, Secretary Tillerson visited Turkey to discuss the campaign against ISIS in Raqqa. The final assault on Raqqa has stalled over a disagreement on which forces to use. The U.S. would prefer to see Raqqa taken by a coalition of Arab and Kurdish YPG units, collectively known as the Syrian Democratic Forces. Because Turkey considers the YPG an extension of the banned PKK, the Turkish Government is proposing to use its own military and a mix of local Arab partners to take back Raqqa.

Since the SDF has proven to be a reliable force on the ground in Syria and given no viable alternative, the United States will most likely back the SDF option. However, it appears to be waiting for the outcome of Turkey's referendum before making any announcement.

While President Erdogan would have additional control over the Turkish military if the referendum passes, it is unclear how he will react to this decision. The buildup to the referendum has also instigated worrying diplomatic roads between Europe and Turkey. The tension between these two critical partners of the U.S. may result in long-term damage to Turkey's EU prospects and to NATO's common defense community.

If emboldened by a victory, President Erdogan may seek to test Europe's limits further and bring Turkey's EU candidacy to a halt. A loss in the referendum fueled by conspiracies about European intervention may be just as detrimental. Regardless, NATO allies will need to work to steady relations between all partners.

The outcome of the Turkish referendum can also impact regional energy cooperation. The dynamic of Turkey's influence on the Cyprus reunification process and the negotiations' implications on the eastern Mediterranean's gas reserves is of note. A successful referendum could empower some Turkish nationalists in the MHP who helped usher the package through Parliament in January. Their views on Cyprus and the Turkish military presence there may spoil a potential agreement.

It is not clear if President Erdogan will follow MHP's lead after the referendum. What is clear, however, is that once the referendum is over, Turkey will have more time and attention to focus on Cyprus. If a deal is reached, reconciliation between Turkish and Greek Cypriots can occur, and Mediterranean gas can flow into the European market.

The last two international considerations surrounding Turkey's referendum are economic prosperity and democratic ideals, which go hand in hand. Turkey experienced growth and economic stability early on under President Erdogan. Recently, the AK Party government's indifference toward democratic institutions, rule of law, and freedom of expression has undercut Turkey's lasting prosperity.

It is difficult to foresee how a consolidation of power away from the judiciary and into the executive would enhance the democratic principles needed for an open trade-based economy. The only way to bring about more certainty in the Turkish economy is if checks and balances are restored and maintained.

Turkey has always been strongest when it comes close to the ideal of a liberal democratic society where all voices are tolerated. For this reason, Turkey's partners must address challenges to democratic norms head on. Only direct U.S. engagement, a true partnership, and conversation about Turkey's commitment to democratic ideals can deter worse behavior, enhance global security, and bring Turkey to the table on critical issues.

In order to be taken seriously, the West must also hold true to its own democratic values and principles. If attacks against the press, unethical behavior, or disregard for democratic institutions becomes commonplace, it will be difficult to make the case of their importance in Turkey and other countries.

Mr. Chairman, Ranking Member Meeks, members of this committee, thank you again for your careful attention to U.S.-Turkey relations. I look forward to your questions.

[The prepared statement of Ms. Durakoglu follows:]

 **Atlantic Council**

Turkey's Democracy Under Challenge

April 5, 2017

Prepared statement by

Naz Durakoglu

Senior Fellow and Strategist, Digital Forensic Research Lab, The Atlantic Council

Before the

The United States House Committee on Foreign Affairs

United States House of Representatives
115th Congress

49

Atlantic Council

Thank you Chairman Rohrabacher, Ranking Member Meeks, and members of the Committee for the opportunity to join you and discuss Turkey's upcoming constitutional referendum. It is an honor to testify before you both as a witness, and a former staffer on this Committee under Congressman William R. Keating.

As this Committee knows, the United States and Turkey share one of the most complex, yet significant partnerships within the North Atlantic Treaty Organization (NATO). This critically important relationship has withstood both positive turning points and challenging decisions taken by both countries. In this way, the Turkish referendum on April 16 should not be viewed as a stand-alone, domestic event — rather, a critical moment in Turkey's history with wider implications for the transatlantic community and the NATO Alliance.

The referendum vote comes at a time of heightened fear, polarization, and trauma for Turks, who have endured one of the deadliest years in their recent history with a string of high-casualty terrorist attacks and a failed coup on July 15. As the country reels from the devastation of these repeated blows, Turkish citizens are increasingly affected by a forceful, post-coup crackdown against thousands in Turkey, including foreigners, well-respected journalists, businessmen, public servants, and academics.

This environment colors the 18-article constitutional package at the center of the referendum, which if passed, would transform Turkey's parliamentary political structure into a presidential system with few checks and balances. Amid allegations of improper voting procedures and physical altercations, Turkey's parliament passed this package of amendments on January 21 once Turkish President Recep Tayyip Erdogan's ruling AK-Party teamed up with members from Turkey's nationalist opposition party, the MHP.

The package includes fundamental changes to the Turkish political system that would: 1) eliminate the position of the prime minister and render the president the head of state, head of government, and head of ruling party; 2) grant presidential authority to appoint cabinet ministers and two-thirds of the country's senior judges; 3) permit the executive to pass laws by decree, dismiss parliament, and declare a state of emergency; 4) empower the current president to call early presidential and parliamentary elections, and possibly open the door to an Erdogan presidency until 2029.

Given the uncertainty over Turkey's future, the population remains split on the referendum and on President Erdogan's policies and response to the instability gripping the nation. While many ruling AK-Party supporters continue to see President Erdogan as a strong, calming force in a volatile region, others in the country view his policies as a vehicle for chaos and blame him for Turkey's declining prosperity and security.

Internationally, Turkey's partners and allies have been largely silent, despite accusations from Turkish officials charging Europeans with attempting to influence the referendum. No matter the outcome, Turkey's partners — particularly the United States — must prepare to engage with a Turkish state that is in a battle for its future. It is not only the referendum's outcome that matters, but President Erdogan's governance style and how the Turkish leadership chooses to move Turkey beyond the post-coup phase. The four key areas in which U.S.-Turkey relations will be affected by decisions made after the referendum are: transatlantic security, energy cooperation, economic prosperity, and last but not

Atlantic Council

least, democratic values.

Having the second largest military in the NATO alliance, Turkey already has a profound influence on international security matters. The use of Turkey's Incirlik Air Base, according to U.S. Secretary of State Rex Tillerson, allows for 25 percent more strikes against ISIS in Syria, and much of the United States' humanitarian aid work in Syria is based out of southeastern Turkey. Moreover, Turkey's location between Iran, Iraq, Syria, Europe, and the Caucasus puts Turkey at the center of some of the most unstable, yet critical hotspots in the world. Indeed, modern Turkey still maintains the age-old characterization of Turkey as a strategic friend in a troubled neighborhood.

Last week, Secretary Tillerson visited Turkey to "build on three mutual long-term goals: working together to defeat Daesh/ISIS; building stability in the region; and bolstering economic ties between [the] two nations." His visit came on the heels of advanced planning stages in the campaign against ISIS in Raqqa. The final assault on Raqqa has stalled over a disagreement on which forces the United States should use to liberate and hold the ISIS stronghold. The United States would prefer to see Raqqa taken by a coalition of Arab and Kurdish Popular Protection Units (YPG), collectively known as the Syrian Defense Forces (SDF). However, because Turkey considers the YPG an extension of the banned Kurdistan Workers' Party or PKK — the latter designated as a terrorist entity by the U.S. government —they are proposing to use their own military and a mix of local, Arab partners to take back Raqqa. It is not clear, however, whether Turkey can adequately muster these forces beyond its recently-stalled Euphrates Shield operation.

Since the SDF has proven to be a reliable force on the ground in Syria, and given no viable alternative absent a major influx of U.S. troops, the United States has little choice but to back the SDF option. However, it appears to be waiting for the outcome of Turkey's referendum before making any announcement. While President Erdogan would have additional control over the Turkish military if the referendum passes, it is unclear what options Turkey has to prevent the SDF from taking Raqqa. President Erdogan's flexibility toward a U.S. decision to use SDF forces may change after the referendum, but it is difficult to predict his response. Regardless, it may be a turning point for relations and an area to closely watch.

The growing rift between Turkey and Europe is also a worrying trend in transatlantic security as it threatens to unravel a delicate balance between these two crucial partners. President Erdogan has already threatened to undo the deal that the EU and Turkey struck at the height of the refugee crisis in 2016. The agreement — while imperfect — stipulates that irregular migrants entering Greece can be returned to Turkey in exchange for expedited visa liberalization for Turks, a €3 billion assistance package, and speedy processing of refugees waiting to enter Europe from Turkey. Unfortunately, the EU has reluctantly complied with its part of the bargain, and Turkey, which already generously hosts 3 million refugees, finds its patience wavering.

The build-up to the referendum has already instigated intense diplomatic rows as some European nations blocked Turkish officials from campaigning on their territory, and Ankara reacted with accusations of Nazism and threats to reevaluate its relationship with Europe. The undoing of decorum between Europe and Turkey may result in long-term damage to Turkey's EU prospects and to NATO's common defense community, which demands consensus on decisions. If emboldened by a

Atlantic Council

victory, President Erdogan may seek to test Europe's limits even further and bring Turkey's EU candidacy to a halt, making for a very uncomfortable NATO Alliance. A loss in the referendum, fueled by conspiracies about European intervention, may be just as detrimental to the fraying Turkey-EU relationship. Regardless, NATO Allies will need to work to steady relations between these partners.

The outcome of the Turkish referendum can also impact energy cooperation with Europe for the same reasons that threaten transatlantic security. Yet, there is the added dynamic of Turkey's influence on the Cyprus reunification process and the negotiations' implications on the Eastern Mediterranean's gas reserves.

While Turkey has pledged to be a constructive force in this difficult process, a successful referendum could empower Turkish nationalists in the MHP who supported the ruling AK party and ushered the constitutional package through parliament in January. The nationalists have not staked out a position on negotiations, but their traditional views on Cyprus and the Turkish military's presence there may spoil a potential agreement and endanger this unique opportunity. It is not clear, however, if President Erdogan would follow MHP's lead after the referendum takes place. What is clear is that once the referendum is over, Turkey will have more time and attention to focus on Cyprus. If a deal is reached, reconciliation between Turkish and Greek Cypriots can finally come to fruition after decades of attempts, and Mediterranean gas can flow into the European market, helping to reduce Europe's dependence on Russian gas.

Similarly, referendum politics may affect ongoing plans between Turkey and Russia to build a second natural gas pipeline in the TurkStream project. This pipeline would bring Gazprom gas to Europe by bypassing Ukraine. A win in the referendum may help President Erdogan push the project along, despite environmental concerns at home and foreign policy implications for Ukraine.

The last two international considerations surrounding Turkey's referendum are economic prosperity and democratic ideals — which as Turkey's example shows go hand in hand. Turkey experienced growth and economic stability throughout President Erdogan's time in office, but more recently, the AK Party government's indifference toward democratic institutions, rule of law, freedom of expression, and media has undercut Turkey's lasting prosperity. Already, the Turkish Lira has experienced a sharp decline, making it the worst emerging market currency in 2017. This reflects market fears over Turkey's slowing economy and rising inflation. The business climate is greatly affected by uncertainty in Turkey, which is already experiencing capital flight and a reluctance by foreigners to invest. Turkey has the world's 17th largest economy, and any instability will have major implications for neighbors throughout the region. Post-referendum, no matter the outcome, the Turkish government must work to maintain checks and balances and help steady the climate to encourage investment and growth, once again.

Another issue that the Turkish government must pay attention to is any instance of foreign travelers or residents being caught up in the post-coup crackdown. These examples are growing and hurting economic prospects for Turkey. For example, the arrest of long-time resident of Turkey and U.S. citizen, Pastor Andrew Brunson, reverberates throughout the United States and has led to Secretary Tillerson, and previously Secretary John Kerry, to raise this case repeatedly with Turkish officials. Cases like Pastor Brunson's do not encourage a strong investment climate and do even less to help

Atlantic Council

generate tourism in Turkey.

It is difficult to foresee how a consolidation of power away from the judiciary and into the executive would improve investment potential in Turkey or enhance the democratic principles needed for an open, trade-based economy. The only way for the referendum to bring about more certainty in the Turkish economy is if checks and balances are restored and maintained under the new Turkish presidency or any political system.

Regardless of the outcome of the referendum, Turkey has always been strongest when it comes close to the ideal of a liberal democratic society such as during the earlier years of the Erdogan administration. Turkey's partners must address challenges to democratic norms head-on. Speaking out on these matters directly should not be done in a way that embarrasses Turkish officials or through one-off press statements or criticisms. Instead, the most effective means of communicating concerns is to maintain close high-level contacts between Turkey and the United States. Only direct U.S. engagement, a true partnership, and conversations about Turkey's commitment to democratic ideals can deter worse behavior, protect our own security, and bring Turkey to the table on critical international issues.

To achieve these goals, the United States and the West must also hold true to their own democratic values and principles at home. If attacks against the press, unethical behavior, or disregard for democratic institutions become commonplace among Western leaders, it will be difficult to make the case for their importance to Turkey and other countries.

Mr. Chairman, Ranking Member Meeks, members of this Committee, thank you for your careful attention to the future of Turkey and U.S.-Turkish relations. I look forward to your questions.

Thank you.

Mr. ROHRABACHER. And thank all of you for your testimony today.

The Chairman will start the questions, and then we will proceed with the rest of the members.

Let me start. The contrast between our two central witnesses here was dramatic in terms of the picture that was being painted.

Let me just ask: Mr. Cinar, you mentioned that freedom of expression and the press in Turkey is something that Turkish people cherish and over the years have expected to live with, and there are certain guarantees of that freedom. But yet you did recognize that, today, there has been a wave of suppression, freedom of speech. There has been a wave of destruction, freedom of the press, but you mentioned you really put that fault on the state of emergency, which is a result of the coup attempt.

My question for you, Mr. Cinar, is, what about the newspapers that were closed up and the journalists that were arrested and kicked out of their job long before the coup? We have been hearing reports. This committee has had a number of hearings on Turkey. I have always tried to be fair, make sure both sides are represented, but we had testimony in our very first hearing on Turkey long before the coup attempt.

So how can you excuse the suppression of freedom of the press and expression, excuse it by saying "the coup" and blaming that on the military then when it was happening long before there was a coup? Go right ahead.

Mr. CINAR. Chairman, that is a great question.

I mean, the freedom of press, yes, Turkey has some problems on freedom of press, but investigations aren't due to their journalistic work but due to their support and link to terrorist organizations. So, when you look at, overall, some journalists and reporters are making propaganda of Fethullah Gulen before the coup and as well as PKK terrorist organization, and also some of the journalists also were sharing intelligence information to the public, which is illegal through the Constitution.

And, also, I would like to highlight as an example journalist newspapers like Zaman. In 2010, there were some cases to the secular groups, and some of the secular journalists were in prison and set up with FETO. Most of them are jailed for many years. At that time, right now, the Gulenists are complaining about freedom of press, but in 2010 and before, the Gulenists newspapers be quiet, and they were supportive of the freedom of press.

So it seems like there is a double standard on what kind of freedom of press we are understanding. As I said, and I would like to give an example. Several thousand newspapers and journalists——

Mr. ROHRABACHER. Mr. Cinar, we will submit that for the record.

Mr. CINAR. Sure.

Mr. ROHRABACHER. And let me just note that someone else's double standard doesn't excuse the current government's suppression before and after the coup of freedom of the press. Because someone else had a double standard doesn't mean that is an excuse.

Mr. CINAR. I totally agree, Chairman. I mean, as I said from my—at the beginning, there are some problems on freedom of speech, but when you look at, overall, 7,000 newspapers and journalists, 200 TV stations, 1,000 radio stations, I mean, still there is freedom at some point that Turkey is operating and journalists are able to criticize President Erdogan and his party. But the reporters or journalists are linked to terrorist organizations; they are face, you know, to crime.

Mr. ROHRABACHER. Some may well be linked because someone has made that report and claimed a link. We have had four hearings on this now, and in the original hearings, what became clear is that certain journalists had lost their jobs shortly after they had reported on corruption of President Erdogan's family and appointees, which does not just jive with an excuse that there is not an overall attempt to suppress speech.

To your knowledge, were there people who were reporting corruption in the Erdogan government? Were they arrested in the beginning and kicked out of their job?

Mr. CINAR. I mean, my understanding is—I am not well knowledge on this, that I can't say there was a corruption or not.

Mr. ROHRABACHER. Okay. You can't answer that. All right. Well, let's go back. Just to be fair, Mr. Phillips, you mentioned that women were now being allowed to wear the hijab in a government office, and before they haven't been permitted. I don't think that is an indication of radical Islam: Letting women make a choice.

Now, if they were forced to wear the hijab and they were forced to do that, that would be a sign that the people had gone overboard and that that was radical Islam.

But, Mr. Phillips, do you have data that suggests that President Erdogan and his regime have actually sold oil from Syria. Are you trying to suggest to us today—and please say it outright if you can—that under Erdogan, the Turkish Government has been pro- viding the resources to terrorist organizations that have been mur- dering people throughout the Middle East?

Mr. PHILLIPS. Yes, that is precisely what I am saying. There were 57,000 emails that had been released linking the Erdogan family directly to the sale of ISIS-controlled oil.

Mr. ROHRABACHER. And that money went to do what?

Mr. PHILLIPS. That money, which totaled, at its peak, $3 million a day, went to ISIS to support its caliphate operations, which is used to kill people and to target Westerners.

Mr. ROHRABACHER. And do you think that, Mr. Cinar's observations—his right to his opinion—but do you think that the fact that you just stated, meaning money that is being syphoned off by the very top of the government and going to terrorists, do you think that had anything to with Erdogan's decision to suppress certain news outlets and to make sure that the press was notified that there would be a price to pay if certain criticism was heard?

Mr. PHILLIPS. Any journalist in Turkey who reports on corruption linking the family to ISIS activities is assured of losing their job and going to jail. We saw that in the case of the Cumhuriyet editor in chief and their foreign affairs editor, both of whom received more than 5-year sentences for reporting on the national intelligence agency's transfer of weapons to Islamic State fighters across the jihadi highway from Sanliurfa to Raqqa, which was a well-known fact, extensively documented.

Mr. ROHRABACHER. I will move on to Mr. Meeks, but let me just thank the witnesses. I think I may have a second round, but better get my colleagues their first round.

Mr. MEEKS. Thank you, Mr. Chairman.

Let me start with Ms. Durakoglu. Now, foreign policy is very difficult, and Turkey is in a very difficult part of the world, and I am trying to figure out with interrelationships with other governments, and et cetera, how we can make sure that the best interest of the United States and actually the best interest of others, whether it is the—those in NATO and EU, how we figure this thing out.

I am really concerned about—because I think your testimony was absolutely correct, that if I am to stand true to myself, I can't ignore human rights violations and individuals being penalized and put in prison without due process or anything of that nature. But I can't advocate for Turkey to be removed from NATO or anything of that nature because they are a vital ally, especially in that region.

So, in your opinion, is there any low-hanging fruit in a U.S.-Turkey cooperation and the political security or economic fronts, something that we can do? You know, because Syria is right there, and we will talk about Syria and talk about—that is my second question. Let me just ask that first.

Ms. DURAKOGLU. Thank you for your question. I think your question actually hits the complexity of the relationship. You are absolutely right. There are definitely serious domestic concerns within Turkey. However, there is reason for the United States and for NATO, in particular, which Turkey is an ally, to be cooperating at all times. Part of it is the geographic location of Turkey itself.

In terms of your question about low-hanging fruit, before I mention that, I would just say President Erdogan has demonstrated that he appreciates continual contact with other leaders. And sometimes I think in the structure that Turkey represents at this point, the message that we might be sending as the United States over to Turkey may not be making its way up. So direct communication is key, even though it might be uncomfortable at times.

In terms of low-hanging fruit, I alluded to this in my testimony, but what seems to be at the forefront of our relationship with Turkey at the moment is what is going to happen with the Raqqa campaign in Syria, and the United States is moving in a direction to work with the Syrian Democratic Forces, which does include YPG elements, which Turkey is highly uncomfortable with.

I think some communication there, more regular contact. Secretary Tillerson was just in Turkey to be able to discuss this. However, without an end game or an end point in Syria on our side, it is difficult to imagine what is going to end up happening with Raqqa, with the forces the United States may choose to use there. So it is difficult to explain to a NATO ally like Turkey that we are going to go ahead with this option; however, we don't necessarily know what is going to come of it, and you obviously have serious concerns.

So I think closer communication is definitely key, and then, of course, economic cooperation. This is something that the Turks raise often, I know, here in Congress as well. That could also be helpful.

But continually raising the issues of Turkey's domestic politics and the people that are being persecuted unnecessarily, that is key, too. That can't be ignored.

Mr. MEEKS. So we have got have those face-to-face honest dialogues with our allies.

Ms. DURAKOGLU. Absolutely.

Mr. MEEKS. When we think they are wrong and when we think they are right.

You mentioned Syria. You know, as the chemical weapons were released yesterday, that is concerning to me. This is complicated stuff, and I don't think that the United States can do—I didn't think that, under President Obama—and I know you worked during the Obama administration—I don't think that he could have done anything by himself or in this country, nor do I think that Donald Trump can.

So the question then becomes the relationships that—in the region. So I believe it was Turkey that shot down a Russian jet some time ago. And so what is the relationship now between Turkey and Russia and Iran and the whole Syria thing? All of that is intertwined. How does that work?

Ms. DURAKOGLU. That is a really interesting question and one that I know Turkey watchers are continually examining, particularly the relationship between Turkey and Russia. The incident you mention happened in November 2015 where the Russian warplane was shot down when it impeded Turkish airspace. And it led to a break in relations between Turkey and Russia and very heated talk. Sanctions actually came into play as well.

Since then, I know that President Erdogan around June 2016 extended an olive branch. They tried to make things better. To be quite frank, the situation—the energy situation in Turkey demands that they do have a sort of cooperation as well as the tourism industry. There are a lot of Russian tourists that go to Turkey.

So I know that Russia and Turkey are working on that relationship. They have had four high-level meetings, most recently earlier in March as well. And that is what we were talking about earlier. Russians are offering them more economic cooperation. There are discussions about Syria. However, when you look on the ground in Syria, suddenly there is a very different picture where Russians are obviously not cooperating with the Turks. So I don't know how long that relationship between Turkey and Russia will last.

Mr. PHILLIPS. Mr. Meeks, could I add to that answer, please?

Mr. MEEKS. All right.

Mr. PHILLIPS. I would like to recognize that the North Atlantic Council established something called a Membership Compliance Review. There are very strict criteria for getting into NATO. There is no process for kicking anybody out. Annually, each member of NATO should be subject to review of their democracy and human rights practices, and if they receive a failing score for 2 years in a row, then their membership should be suspended. This wouldn't only affect countries likes Turkey, but also Hungary would also be under review.

And on the subject of Incirlik that we have heard so much about, yes, Incirlik is an important forward air base, but there are other options. Turkey always holds Incirlik use over our heads. There are bases in Jordan, in Kuwait, in Iraqi Kurdistan. There are British bases in Cyprus. So we can diversify our combat air operations without losing our capacity in the fight against ISIS.

Mr. MEEKS. Thank you.

I am out of time.

Mr. ROHRABACHER. Thank you very much.

Mr. Sires.

Mr. SIRES. Thank you, Mr. Chairman.

You know, I always think that Turkey has this attitude. If we support an Armenian resolution—and I remember when we had the resolution here in Congress, the pressure that was borne, some of the people that supported it, you would think you were going to go to jail.

If you support arming the Kurdish fighters that are fighting ISIS, there is going to be dire consequences. And if you don't return Gulen, they are going to make the U.S. disappear.

I really think that, Mr. Cinar, when you talk about jailing or purging one-third of the journalists in the country, it is a little strong.

I mean, this reminds me of my country when I was a boy. When the Communists took over, this is how they started. So, to me, I mean, this is somebody grabbing for power, and you have this effort where they took over 600 businesses. I mean, what did the businesses have with these generals? To me, it looks like somebody went out there and tried to get some of the better businesses for some of the family members or themselves. So there is just a couple of things here that do not jive in my point of view.

And as far as NATO is concerned, I would hate to depend on Turkey in a crunch the way they have been moving the last few years.

And, Mr. Phillips, my question to you is, if this resolution, if this amendment to the Constitution does not pass, where do you—you know, which I doubt it is not going the pass, from what I am hearing, where do you see Turkey going?

Mr. PHILLIPS. There are 12 credible public opinion polls that have been taken about the referendum. Eight of them say that the "no" campaign is going to win. If, in fact, the votes are stolen or there is an international opinion that the conditions for the referendum were not free and fair, this is going to fuel divisions in Turkey, and we could see social cohesion fall apart and violence become widespread.

That is why it is important for international monitors to be on the ground to verify the voting conditions. We also have to recognize that if this referendum is approved one way or another, Turkey's aspirations of joining the EU are over. It will not be a European country. It will be increasingly inward looking. And as Turkey becomes inward looking, it will be less reliable to the United States. We always talk about Turkey's role fighting the Islamic State. I think that this is a misnomer. We need to recognize that Turkey hasn't fought the Islamic State; it has abetted the Islamic State with money, with weapons, with health care, all of which is well documented. We need to see things as they are, not as we wish them to be or how they used to be.

Mr. SIRES. Mr. Cinar, where do you see Turkey going if this fails?

Mr. CINAR. Congressman, first of all, for the human rights, I would like to give you some examples before I jump to where Turkey is going. And also we need to respect the Turkish people. There is a government that is democratically elected, and the referendum is coming up, including all opposition parties right now. The election is going to be crystal clear, and everybody needs to respect the election.

Regarding the human rights——

Mr. SIRES. So you are comfortable that this is going to be an honest election?

Mr. CINAR. Yes.

Mr. SIRES. There is not going to be any interference by the Erdogan government?

Mr. CINAR. Correct. In the last election, the November election, Congressman, all opposition parties agreed it was a noncorrupted election.

Regarding the human rights, as I submitted——

Mr. SIRES. No Russian interference in the election?

Mr. CINAR. Hopefully not.

Let me talk about human rights and freedom of press. As an example, before the coup, July 13, one of the Gulen journalists, said, "Busted in bed, hung by dawn." Or another one: "You just wait and see what is to come." Another one: "Good times are just around the corner. How I wish I were a colonel today and not professor. Then I would have much more to contribute to this process."

Mr. SIRES. What am I looking at here?

Mr. CINAR. So these are the journalists of Gulen. So they were promoting the coup.

Mr. ROHRABACHER. Unfortunately, votes have just been called. Could you please put those in for the record of this hearing?

Mr. CINAR. Sure.

Mr. ROHRABACHER. We will submit that.

We have about 15 minutes at the most. So we have 10 minutes. I would ask my colleagues to have about 3 minutes each for their questions. We will try to get you in.

Mr. KEATING. Actually, Mr. Cicilline was here first.

Mr. CICILLINE. No, Mr. Keating was.

Mr. ROHRABACHER. Mr. Keating, go right ahead. You have the time. Quit being too gentlemanly.

Mr. KEATING. I think that Ms. Durakoglu made four pillars, if you will, that we should be focused on. My discussions with representatives of Turkey since I have been in Congress have really come back to economic cooperation. There was a great deal of interest when there was interest in the TTIP agreement. Every discussion I had virtually centered on that.

Now, with the failure of our trade agreements, I do hope there is a chance for even a bilateral EU and U.S. agreement. How important would that be, really, to find some inducement for Turkey to have more open discussions with the West and with the U.S.?

Ms. DURAKOGLU. Thank you, Congressman.

That is hugely important. You are 100 percent right. And I know you were very active on that issue at the time. I think, at the time,

59

Turkey was nervous about the TTIP agreement and being left out of the economic prosperity that might take place. But there was a parallel conversation with Turkey about how they can potentially benefit. And they were engaged, and the United States was engaged in that conversation as well. So, as long as that carrot is there, that is very important to bring Turkey to the table, because I am of the opinion, with all due respect to all the viewpoints represented here, that are very important, but they need to continually be more exposed to our ideals as well as our thinking and to be able to understand that we do want what is in the best interest of Turkey, including more freedoms for their people there.

Mr. KEATING. Is there any way to ascertain what the feeling of the Turkish people, what it really was about the coup itself? We heard so much about the coup. But what about people, the general population? Is there any way to get a sense of how they perceived that?

Ms. DURAKOGLU. Yes. There have been several polls. And, unfortunately, there is not a very positive picture to paint there. A lot of the polls—they do overwhelmingly believe that this was a Gulen-orchestrated coup. And many—and, unfortunately, I don't have the exact figure with me—but many also believe that either the Central Intelligence Agency or the United States was behind this, which is wrong across the board. But that is a prevailing view, unfortunately, in Turkey.

Mr. KEATING. I will yield because of the rollcall. Thank you.

Mr. ROHRABACHER. Mr. Cicilline?

Mr. CICILLINE. Thank you. Ms. Durakoglu, I appreciated your testimony, other than that reference to how Mr. Keating inspired you.

Thank you to the witnesses.

What I am interested to know is, with respect to the treatment of journalists and academics and opposition leaders, Mr. Phillips, would you just tell us what your assessment is with respect to the imprisonment of journalists and the conditions in which they are being imprisoned and whether in fact they are primarily people who have disclosed classified documents and the like? What is the real situation in Turkey right now with respect to opposition leaders and journalists?

Mr. PHILLIPS. Freedom House says there is no press freedom. According to Freedom House, Turkey does not have press freedom. Turkey uses legislation as the basis for arresting journalists. The idea that almost 2,000 journalists would have been arrested because they insulted the President to me represents a crackdown on freedom of expression. Using items in the penal code and the Anti-Terror Act to suppress debate is also a violation of freedom of expression.

So we should just deal with the facts. Right now, more journalists are in jail in Turkey than in any other country in the world, more than China, more than Iran. A third of the journalists in the world who are in jail are in jail in Turkey. What conditions they are experiencing there, I can't say. But I do know that the rule of law in Turkey is an instrument to suppress oppositionists.

Mr. CICILLINE. Thank you.

The other question I have is you did a significant amount of research about the role of Turkey both in assisting with logistics and transportation, support and training of ISIS fighters. Could you speak a little bit to that?

And then my last question to other members of the panel is, what is the likelihood that in the context of the continued state of emergency that a referendum can be held which is free and fair and something upon which the international community and the Turkish people can rely?

Mr. PHILLIPS. So we were not able to use primary sources for our research because we weren't on the ground in Syria. We used credible secondary sources. We referred to Vice President Joe Biden's remark at Harvard, where he said that Turkey was the primary sponsor of ISIS. And then, through our research teams in Turkey, looking at Turkish language reporting in Europe and in North America, we came up with scores of credible reports that Turkey was involved in providing weapons, financing, logistics, serving wounded warriors in hospitals in Turkey. So there is ample evidence.

Meanwhile, we hear constant protests from President Erdogan that Turkey is being misrepresented. I think the protests should be coming from the United States that Turkey, a NATO ally, is aiding and abetting a terrorist organization.

Mr. ROHRABACHER. Thank you.

Ms. Kelly.

Ms. KELLY. Thank you, Mr. Chair.

Ms.—I hope it pronounce it right—Durakoglu?

Ms. DURAKOGLU. That is right.

Ms. KELLY. I am concerned with, after the constitutional referendum, I am concerned with the weakening of the independent branches of government because there are few checks and balances in place now. And, also, how will the minority populations be affected, as well as will there be any effect on military independence?

Ms. DURAKOGLU. Thank you, Congresswoman.

Yes, that is a concern. It is also a concern expressed by the Venice Commission that looked at the package of amendments. In terms of the judiciary, I think that some of the greatest changes in the constitutional package take place there. As I alluded to in my testimony, about two-thirds of Turkey's senior judges can now be appointed by the President. And, further, there is a body that actually deals with both prosecutors and judges in Turkey. And they end up dealing with judiciary issues, as well as appointing judges, and the President can appoint a significant amount of those members as well.

That all being said, there have been some studies on the referendum and the package of amendments, and some of them in English actually. And there is the potential to still abide by checks and balances. It really does come down to the President under this new Presidency to be able to maintain that balance. So I know that there are some with the hope that President Erdogan, who will most likely be the President under this new system, be able do that. But when you look at it on paper and all those who have analyzed it, they have a rather bleak view of the separation.

And for minority issues, I would defer to my colleague from the HDP.

Mr. YUKSEL. The situation is very hard because, especially with this situation, they shut down the television, which was transmitting only cartoons for the children in Kurdish. And after a lot of pressure, they allowed. So, even with a lot of translation in Turkish, or should be more than 60 percent in Turkish, that is how the minorities live right now, on the front of an assimilation. And other minorities numerically are less, and they are under huge pressure. And, plus, the Alawites in Turkey are under huge pressure because they see the regime changing more and more as an Islamic regime and without any law, like Iran, and they are afraid that they will be the next target.

Mr. CINAR. Congresswoman?

Mr. ROHRABACHER. Excuse me. You got your minute because you are here, and we appreciate you giving the other side. But we are going to have to be out of here in a couple minutes. So 1 minute. What do you got?

Mr. CINAR. Sure. Congresswoman, Chairman, I wish at least we can see a little bit appreciation of Turkey's fight against ISIS. And I will be submitting some documents that U.S. Pentagon also said there is no evidence between ISIS and Turkey. And Turkey lost 72 security personnel on the ground and 1,000 ISIS terrorists neutralized by Turkish army in Syria's operation.

And also, regarding the human rights, and I would like to ask you a question, you have a look at some HDP members here that are promoting PKK at their meetings. Can you imagine a Congressman speaking——

Mr. ROHRABACHER. You want to put that in the record?

Mr. CINAR. Sure.

Mr. ROHRABACHER. Okay.

Mr. CINAR. Can you imagine a Congressman attending an ISIS leader's event and promoting the terrorist organization? So this is a big problem for Turkey. It is a national security risk.

Mr. ROHRABACHER. All right. Thank you very much.

I am sorry. We only have got 2 minutes or 3 minutes to go because we have to go vote.

Do you have a 1-minute closing statement, Mr. Meeks?

Mr. MEEKS. I want to say real quickly, number one, I want to thank the witnesses for your testimony. I want to thank the chairman for the diversity of the witnesses that you presented. I think you got thoughts from all sides.

For me, this is a very difficult, difficult period, a difficult decision. A lot to look at. And as I said in my opening statement, the key to me is, the bottom line, the one that I have ultimate belief in is the Turkish people. So I should hope that the Turkish people—that is where I keep my hope—that I will stand with them. I will try to make sure, where I see atrocities, I will speak up and speak out. But I believe that the Turkish people will stand up. And as I have seen the brave ones still on the streets now protesting and doing what they think is necessary and others who may be on the other side, because ultimately that is what makes the difference, the Turkish people.

Mr. ROHRABACHER. Thank you, Mr. Meeks.

And I would echo that sentiment. The Turkish people are voting on whether they want to have a tough, strong, centralized power controlling their government or whether they want to have more of a loose freedom and exchange. Obviously, we don't think they should overlook this incredible suppression of the press and of disagreements and dissidents that now is in place in Turkey as compared to the last 15 or 20 years in Turkey's history. Let me note that one of my colleagues said we don't know if we can rely on Turkish people to back us up. The bottom line: The whole Cold War, the Turkish people were the friends of the United States. We could count on them. They fought in Korea. They were part of the deterrent that prevented the Soviet Union from thinking they could come down and attack all of Europe.

The Turkish people are going to the polls right now to decide, will they be friends of the West and the United States? Will they be a friend of the United States? And will they have a radical-oriented government, an Islamic-oriented government, a terrorist-oriented government in power in Turkey, or will they be friends of the United States and have more of a democratic future? That will be determined.

I agree with Mr. Meeks; we are on the side of the people of Turkey. Please, I would hope that they hear our plea, remain our friend. Don't go to the polls and then basically join in this negation of a friendship that has lasted so long and done so much well for the people of the United States and the people of Turkey.

With that, I say thank you very much. We have to go vote.

[Whereupon, at 3:34 p.m., the subcommittee was adjourned.]

APPENDIX

64

SUBCOMMITTEE HEARING NOTICE
COMMITTEE ON FOREIGN AFFAIRS
U.S. HOUSE OF REPRESENTATIVES
WASHINGTON, DC 20515-6128

Subcommittee on Europe, Eurasia, and Emerging Threats
Dana Rohrabacher (R-CA), Chairman

March 30, 2017

TO: **MEMBERS OF THE COMMITTEE ON FOREIGN AFFAIRS**

You are respectfully requested to attend an OPEN hearing of the Committee on Foreign Affairs, to be held by the Subcommittee on Europe, Eurasia, and Emerging Threats in Room 2172 of the Rayburn House Office Building (and available live on the Committee website at http://www.ForeignAffairs.house.gov):

DATE: Wednesday, April 5, 2017

TIME: 2:00 p.m.

SUBJECT: Turkey's Democracy Under Challenge

WITNESSES: Mr. David L. Phillips
               Director
               Program on Peace-Building and Rights
               Institute for the Study of Human Rights
               Columbia University

               Mr. Mehmet Yuksel
               Representative to the United States
               People's Democratic Party in Turkey

               Mr. Ali Cinar
               President
               Turkish Heritage Organization

               Ms. Naz Durakoglu
               Senior Fellow
               Digital Forensic Research Lab
               Atlantic Council

By Direction of the Chairman

COMMITTEE ON FOREIGN AFFAIRS

MINUTES OF SUBCOMMITTEE ON _____*Europe, Eurasia, and Emerging Threats*_____ HEARING

Day___*Wednesday*___ Date___*April 5, 2017*___ Room___*2172 RHOB*___

Starting Time ___*2:18 p.m.*___ Ending Time ___*3:34 p.m.*___

Recesses ⎹ *0* ⎹ (___to ___) (___to ___) (___to ___) (___to ___) (___to ___) (___to ___)

Presiding Member(s)

Rep. Rohrabacher

Check all of the following that apply:

Open Session ☑   Electronically Recorded (taped) ☑
Executive (closed) Session ☐   Stenographic Record ☑
Televised ☐

TITLE OF HEARING:

Turkey's Democracy Under Challenge

SUBCOMMITTEE MEMBERS PRESENT:

Rep. Meeks, Rep. Sherman, Rep. Keating, Rep. Sires, Rep. Cicilline, Rep. Kelly

---

NON-SUBCOMMITTEE MEMBERS PRESENT: *(Mark with an * if they are not members of full committee.)*

N/A

HEARING WITNESSES: Same as meeting notice attached? Yes ☑ No ☐
(If "no", please list below and include title, agency, department, or organization.)

STATEMENTS FOR THE RECORD: *(List any statements submitted for the record.)*

Attached

TIME SCHEDULED TO RECONVENE _____
or
TIME ADJOURNED ___*3:34 p.m.*___

_____
Subcommittee Staff Associate

REVISED STATEMENT SUBMITTED AFTER THE HEARING BY MS. NAZ DURAKOGLU, STRATEGIST AND SENIOR FELLOW, DIGITAL FORENSIC RESEARCH LAB, ATLANTIC COUNCIL

Turkey's Democracy Under Challenge

April 5, 2017

Updated, prepared statement by

Naz Durakoglu

Senior Fellow and Strategist, Digital Forensic Research Lab, The Atlantic Council

Before the

The United States House Committee on Foreign Affairs
United States House of Representatives
115th Congress

Atlantic Council

Thank you Chairman Rohrabacher, Ranking Member Meeks, and members of the Committee for the opportunity to join you and discuss Turkey's upcoming constitutional referendum. It is an honor to testify before you both as a witness, and a former staffer on this Committee under Congressman William R. Keating.

As this Committee knows, the United States and Turkey share one of the most complex, yet significant partnerships within the North Atlantic Treaty Organization (NATO). This critically important relationship has withstood both positive turning points and challenging decisions taken by both countries. In this way, the Turkish referendum on April 16 should not be viewed as a stand-alone, domestic event — rather, a critical moment in Turkey's history with wider implications for the transatlantic community and the NATO Alliance.

The referendum vote comes at a time of heightened fear, polarization, and trauma for Turks, who have endured one of the deadliest years in their recent history with a string of high-casualty terrorist attacks and a failed coup on July 15. As the country reels from the devastation of these repeated blows, Turkish citizens are increasingly affected by a forceful, post-coup crackdown against thousands in Turkey, including foreigners, well-respected journalists, businessmen, public servants, and academics.

This environment colors the 18-article constitutional package at the center of the referendum, which if passed, would transform Turkey's parliamentary political structure into a presidential system with few checks and balances. Amid allegations of improper voting procedures and physical altercations, Turkey's parliament passed this package of amendments on January 21 once Turkish President Recep Tayyip Erdogan's ruling AK Party teamed up with members from Turkey's nationalist opposition party, the MHP.

The package includes fundamental changes to the Turkish political system that would: 1) eliminate the position of the prime minister and render the president the head of state, head of government, and head of ruling party; 2) grant presidential authority to appoint cabinet ministers and two-thirds of the country's senior judges; 3) permit the executive to pass laws by decree, dismiss parliament, and declare a state of emergency; 4) empower the current president to call early presidential and parliamentary elections, and possibly open the door to an Erdogan presidency until 2029.

Given the uncertainty over Turkey's future, the population remains split on the referendum and on President Erdogan's policies and response to the instability gripping the nation. While many ruling AK-Party supporters continue to see President Erdogan as a strong, calming force in a volatile region, others in the country view his policies as a vehicle for chaos and blame him for Turkey's declining prosperity and security.

Internationally, Turkey's partners and allies have been largely silent, despite accusations from Turkish officials charging Europeans with attempting to influence the referendum. No matter the outcome, Turkey's partners — particularly the United States — must prepare to engage with a Turkish state that is in a battle for its future. It is not only the referendum's outcome that matters, but President Erdogan's governance style and how the Turkish leadership chooses to move Turkey beyond the post-coup phase. The four key areas in which U.S.-Turkey relations will be affected by decisions made after the referendum are: transatlantic security, energy cooperation, economic prosperity, and last but not

Atlantic Council

least, democratic values.

Having the second largest military in the NATO alliance, Turkey already has a profound influence on international security matters. The use of Turkey's Incirlik Air Base, according to U.S. Secretary of State Rex Tillerson, allows for 25 percent more strikes against ISIS in Syria, and much of the United States' humanitarian aid work in Syria is based out of southeastern Turkey. Moreover, Turkey's location between Iran, Iraq, Syria, Europe, and the Caucasus puts Turkey at the center of some of the most unstable, yet critical hotspots in the world. Indeed, modern Turkey still maintains the age-old characterization of Turkey as a strategic friend in a troubled neighborhood.

Last week, Secretary Tillerson visited Turkey to "build on three mutual long-term goals: working together to defeat Daesh/ISIS; building stability in the region; and bolstering economic ties between [the] two nations." His visit came on the heels of advanced planning stages in the campaign against ISIS in Raqqa. The final assault on Raqqa has stalled over a disagreement on which forces the United States should use to liberate and hold the ISIS stronghold. The United States would prefer to see Raqqa taken by a coalition of Arab and Kurdish Popular Protection Units (YPG), collectively known as the Syrian Democratic Forces (SDF). However, because Turkey considers the YPG an extension of the banned Kurdistan Workers' Party or PKK — the latter designated as a terrorist entity by the U.S. government —they are proposing to use their own military and a mix of local, Arab partners to take back Raqqa. It is not clear, however, whether Turkey can adequately muster these forces beyond its recently-stalled Euphrates Shield operation.

Since the SDF has proven to be a reliable force on the ground in Syria, and given no viable alternative absent a major influx of U.S. troops, the United States has little choice but to back the SDF option. However, it appears to be waiting for the outcome of Turkey's referendum before making any announcement. While President Erdogan would have additional control over the Turkish military if the referendum passes, it is unclear what options Turkey has to prevent the SDF from taking Raqqa. President Erdogan's flexibility toward a U.S. decision to use SDF forces may change after the referendum, but it is difficult to predict his response. Regardless, it may be a turning point for relations and an area to closely watch.

The growing rift between Turkey and Europe is also a worrying trend in transatlantic security as it threatens to unravel a delicate balance between these two crucial partners. President Erdogan has already threatened to undo the deal that the EU and Turkey struck at the height of the refugee crisis in 2016. The agreement — while imperfect — stipulates that irregular migrants entering Greece can be returned to Turkey in exchange for expedited visa liberalization for Turks, a €3 billion assistance package, and speedy processing of refugees waiting to enter Europe from Turkey. Unfortunately, the EU has reluctantly complied with its part of the bargain, and Turkey, which already generously hosts 3 million refugees, finds its patience wavering.

The build-up to the referendum has already instigated intense diplomatic rows as some European nations blocked Turkish officials from campaigning on their territory, and Ankara reacted with accusations of Nazism and threats to reevaluate its relationship with Europe. The undoing of decorum between Europe and Turkey may result in long-term damage to Turkey's EU prospects and to NATO's common defense community, which demands consensus on decisions. If emboldened by a

Atlantic Council

victory, President Erdogan may seek to test Europe's limits even further and bring Turkey's EU candidacy to a halt, making for a very uncomfortable NATO Alliance. A loss in the referendum, fueled by conspiracies about European intervention, may be just as detrimental to the fraying Turkey-EU relationship. Regardless, NATO Allies will need to work to steady relations between these partners.

The outcome of the Turkish referendum can also impact energy cooperation with Europe for the same reasons that threaten transatlantic security. Yet, there is the added dynamic of Turkey's influence on the Cyprus reunification process and the negotiations' implications on the Eastern Mediterranean's gas reserves.

While Turkey has pledged to be a constructive force in this difficult process, a successful referendum could empower Turkish nationalists in the MHP who supported the ruling AK party and ushered the constitutional package through parliament in January. The nationalists have not staked out a position on negotiations, but their traditional views on Cyprus and the Turkish military's presence there may spoil a potential agreement and endanger this unique opportunity. It is not clear, however, if President Erdogan would follow MHP's lead after the referendum takes place. What is clear is that once the referendum is over, Turkey will have more time and attention to focus on Cyprus. If a deal is reached, reconciliation between Turkish and Greek Cypriots can finally come to fruition after decades of attempts, and Mediterranean gas can flow into the European market, helping to reduce Europe's dependence on Russian gas.

Similarly, referendum politics may affect ongoing plans between Turkey and Russia to build a second natural gas pipeline in the TurkStream project. This pipeline would bring Gazprom gas to Europe by bypassing Ukraine. A win in the referendum may help President Erdogan push the project along, despite environmental concerns at home and foreign policy implications for Ukraine.

The last two international considerations surrounding Turkey's referendum are economic prosperity and democratic ideals — which as Turkey's example shows go hand in hand. Turkey experienced growth and economic stability throughout President Erdogan's time in office, but more recently, the AK Party government's indifference toward democratic institutions, rule of law, freedom of expression, and media has undercut Turkey's lasting prosperity. Already, the Turkish Lira has experienced a sharp decline, making it the worst emerging market currency in 2017. This reflects market fears over Turkey's slowing economy and rising inflation. The business climate is greatly affected by uncertainty in Turkey, which is already experiencing capital flight and a reluctance by foreigners to invest. Turkey has the world's 17th largest economy, and any instability will have major implications for neighbors throughout the region. Post-referendum, no matter the outcome, the Turkish government must work to maintain checks and balances and help steady the climate to encourage investment and growth, once again.

Another issue that the Turkish government must pay attention to is any instance of foreign travelers or residents being caught up in the post-coup crackdown. These examples are growing and hurting economic prospects for Turkey. For example, the arrest of long-time resident of Turkey and U.S. citizen, Pastor Andrew Brunson, reverberates throughout the United States and has led to Secretary Tillerson, and previously Secretary John Kerry, to raise this case repeatedly with Turkish officials. Cases like Pastor Brunson's do not encourage a strong investment climate and do even less to help

Atlantic Council

generate tourism in Turkey.

It is difficult to foresee how a consolidation of power away from the judiciary and into the executive would improve investment potential in Turkey or enhance the democratic principles needed for an open, trade-based economy. The only way for the referendum to bring about more certainty in the Turkish economy is if checks and balances are restored and maintained under the new Turkish presidency or any political system.

Regardless of the outcome of the referendum, Turkey has always been strongest when it comes close to the ideal of a liberal democratic society where all voices are represented. Turkey's partners must address challenges to democratic norms head-on. Speaking out on these matters directly should not be done in a way that embarrasses Turkish officials or through one-off press statements or criticisms. Instead, the most effective means of communicating concerns is to maintain close high-level contacts between Turkey and the United States. Only direct U.S. engagement, a true partnership, and conversations about Turkey's commitment to democratic ideals can deter worse behavior, protect our own security, and bring Turkey to the table on critical international issues.

To achieve these goals, the United States and the West must also hold true to their own democratic values and principles at home. If attacks against the press, unethical behavior, or disregard for democratic institutions become commonplace among Western leaders, it will be difficult to make the case for their importance to Turkey and other countries.

Mr. Chairman, Ranking Member Meeks, members of this Committee, thank you for your careful attention to the future of Turkey and U.S.-Turkish relations. I look forward to your questions.

Thank you.

MATERIAL SUBMITTED FOR THE RECORD BY MR. DAVID L. PHILLIPS, DIRECTOR, PROGRAM ON PEACE-BUILDING AND RIGHTS, INSTITUTE FOR THE STUDY OF HUMAN RIGHTS, COLUMBIA UNIVERSITY

Research Paper: ISIS-Turkey Links

By David L. Phillips

Introduction

Is Turkey collaborating with the Islamic State (ISIS)? Allegations range from military cooperation and weapons transfers to logistical support, financial assistance, and the provision of medical services. It is also alleged that Turkey turned a blind eye to ISIS attacks against Kobani.

President Recep Tayyip Erdogan and Prime Minister Ahmet Davutoglu strongly deny complicity with ISIS. Erdogan visited the Council on Foreign Relations on September 22, 2014. He criticized "smear campaigns [and] attempts to distort perception about us." Erdogan decried, "A systematic attack on Turkey's international reputation, "complaining that "Turkey has been subject to very unjust and ill-intentioned news items from media organizations." Erdogan posited: "My request from our friends in the United States is to make your assessment about Turkey by basing your information on objective sources."

Columbia University's Program on Peace-building and Rights assigned a team of researchers in the United States, Europe, and Turkey to examine Turkish and international media, assessing the credibility of allegations. This report draws on a variety of international sources — The New York Times, The Washington Post, The Guardian, The Daily Mail, BBC, Sky News, as well as Turkish sources, CNN Turk, Hurriyet Daily News, Taraf, Cumhuriyet, and Radikal among others.

Allegations

Turkey Provides Military Equipment to ISIS

• An ISIS commander told *The Washington Post* on August 12, 2014: "Most of the fighters who joined us in the beginning of the war came via Turkey, and so did our equipment and supplies."

• Kemal Kiliçdaroglu, head of the Republican People's Party (CHP), produced a statement from the Adana Office of the Prosecutor on October 14, 2014 maintaining that Turkey supplied weapons to terror groups. He also produced interview transcripts from truck drivers who delivered weapons to the groups. According to Kiliçdaroglu, the Turkish government claims the trucks were for humanitarian aid to the Turkmen, but the Turkmen said no humanitarian aid was delivered.

• According to CHP Vice President Bulent Tezcan, three trucks were stopped in Adana for inspection on January 19, 2014. The trucks were loaded with weapons in Esenboga Airport in Ankara. The drivers drove the trucks to the border, where a MIT agent was supposed to take over and drive the trucks to Syria to deliver materials to ISIS and groups in Syria. This happened many times. When the trucks were stopped, MIT agents tried to keep the inspectors from looking inside the crates. The inspectors found rockets, arms, and ammunitions.

• Cumhuriyet reports that Fuat Avni, a preeminent Twitter user who reported on the December 17th corruption probe, that audio tapes confirm that Turkey provided financial and military aid to terrorist groups associated with Al Qaeda on October 12, 2014. On the tapes, Erdogan pressured the Turkish Armed Forces to go to war with Syria. Erdogan demanded that Hakan Fidan, the head of Turkey's National Intelligence Agency (MIT), come up with a justification for attacking Syria.

• Hakan Fidan told Prime Minister Ahmet Davutoglu, Yasar Guler, a senior defense official, and Feridun Sinirlioglu, a senior foreign affairs official: "If need be, I'll send 4 men into Syria. I'll formulate a reason to go to war by shooting 8 rockets into Turkey; I'll have them attack the Tomb of Suleiman Shah."

• Documents surfaced on September 19th, 2014 showing that the Saudi Emir Bender Bin Sultan financed the transportation of arms to ISIS through Turkey. A flight leaving Germany dropped off arms in the Etimesgut airport in Turkey, which was then split into three containers, two of which were given to ISIS and one to Gaza.

Turkey Provided Transport and Logistical Assistance to ISIS Fighters

• According to Radikal on June 13, 2014, Interior Minister Muammar Guler signed a directive: "According to our regional gains, we will help al-Nusra militants against the branch of PKK terrorist organization, the PYD, within our borders...Hatay is a strategic location for the mujahideen crossing from within our borders to Syria. Logistical support for Islamist groups will be increased, and their training, hospital care, and safe passage will mostly take place in Hatay...MIT and the Religious Affairs Directorate will coordinate the placement of fighters in public accommodations."

• The Daily Mail reported on August 25, 2014 that many foreign militants joined ISIS in Syria and Iraq after traveling through Turkey, but Turkey did not try to stop them. This article describes how foreign militants, especially from the UK, go to Syria and Iraq through the Turkish border. They call the border the "Gateway to Jihad." Turkish army soldiers either turn a blind eye and let them pass, or the jihadists pay the border guards as little as $10 to facilitate their crossing.

• Britain's Sky News obtained documents showing that the Turkish government has stamped passports of foreign militants seeking to cross the Turkey border into Syria to join ISIS.

• The BBC interviewed villagers, who claim that buses travel at night, carrying jihadists to fight Kurdish forces in Syria and Iraq, not the Syrian Armed Forces.

• A senior Egyptian official indicated on October 9, 2014 that Turkish intelligence is passing satellite imagery and other data to ISIS.

Turkey Provided Training to ISIS Fighters

• CNN Turk reported on July 29, 2014 that in the heart of Istanbul, places like Duzce and Adapazari, have become gathering spots for terrorists. There are religious orders where ISIS militants are trained. Some of these training videos are posted on the Turkish ISIS propaganda website takvahaber.net. According to CNN Turk, Turkish security forces could have stopped these developments if they had wanted to.

• Turks who joined an affiliate of ISIS were recorded at a public gathering in Istanbul, which took place on July 28, 2014.

• A video shows an ISIS affiliate holding a prayer/gathering in Omerli, a district of Istanbul. In response to the video, CHP Vice President, MP Tanrikulu submitted parliamentary questions to the Minister of the Interior, Efkan Ala, asking questions such as, "Is it true that a camp or camps have been allocated to an affiliate of ISIS in Istanbul? What is this affiliate? Who is it made up of? Is the rumor true that the same area allocated for the camp is also used for military exercises?"

• Kemal Kiliçdaroglu warned the AKP government not to provide money and training to terror groups on October 14, 2014. He said, "It isn't right for armed groups to be trained on Turkish soil. You bring foreign fighters to Turkey, put money in their pockets, guns in their hands, and you ask them to kill Muslims in Syria. We told them to stop helping ISIS. Ahmet Davutoglu asked us to show proof. Everyone knows that they're helping ISIS." (See HERE and HERE.)

• According to Jordanian intelligence, Turkey trained ISIS militants for special operations.

Turkey Offers Medical Care to ISIS Fighters

• An ISIS commander told the *Washington Post* on August 12, 2014, "We used to have some fighters — even high-level members of the Islamic State — getting treated in Turkish hospitals."

• Taraf reported on October 12, 2014 that Dengir Mir Mehmet Fırat, a founder of the AKP, said that Turkey supported terrorist groups and still supports them and treats them in hospitals. "In order to weaken the developments in Rojova (Syrian Kurdistan), the government gave concessions and arms to extreme religious groups...the government was helping the wounded. The Minister of Health said something such as, it's a human obligation to care for the ISIS wounded."

• According to Taraf, Ahmet El H, one of the top commanders at ISIS and Al Baghdadi's right hand man, was treated at a hospital in Sanliurfa, Turkey, along with other ISIS militants. The Turkish state paid for their treatment. According to Taraf's sources, ISIS militants are being treated in hospitals all across southeastern Turkey. More and more militants have been coming in to be treated since the start of airstrikes in August. To be more specific, eight ISIS militants were transported through the Sanliurfa border crossing; these are their names: "Mustafa A., Yusuf El R., Mustafa H., Halil El M., Muhammet El H., Ahmet El S., Hasan H., [and] Salim El D."

Turkey Supports ISIS Financially Through Purchase of Oil

• On September 13, 2014, *The New York Times* reported on the Obama administration's efforts to pressure Turkey to crack down on ISIS extensive sales network for oil. James Phillips, a senior fellow at the Heritage Foundation, argues that Turkey has not fully cracked down on ISIS's sales network because it benefits from a lower price for oil, and that there might even be Turks and government officials who benefit from the trade.

• Fehim Taştekin wrote in Radikal on September 13, 2014 about illegal pipelines transporting oil from Syria to nearby border towns in Turkey. The oil is sold for as little as 1.25 liras per liter. Taştekin indicated that many of these illegal pipelines were dismantled after operating for 3 years, once his article was published.

• According to Diken and OdaTV, David Cohen, a Justice Department official, says that there are Turkish individuals acting as middlemen to help sell ISIS's oil through Turkey.

• On October 14, 2014, a German Parliamentarian from the Green Party accused Turkey of allowing the transportation of arms to ISIS over its territory, as well as the sale of oil.

Turkey Assists ISIS Recruitment

• Kemal Kiliçdaroğlu claimed on October 14, 2014 that ISIS offices in Istanbul and Gaziantep are used to recruit fighters. On October 10, 2014, the mufti of Konya said that 100 people from Konya joined ISIS 4 days ago. (See HERE and HERE.)

• OdaTV reports that Takva Haber serves as a propaganda outlet for ISIS to recruit Turkish-speaking individuals in Turkey and Germany. The address where this propaganda website is registered corresponds to the address of a school called Irfan Koleji, which was established by Ilim Yayma Vakfi, a foundation that was created by Erdogan and Davutoglu, among others. It is thus claimed that the propaganda site is operated from the school of the foundation started by AKP members.

• Minister of Sports, Suat Kilic, an AKP member, visited Salafi jihadists who are ISIS supporters in Germany. The group is known for reaching out to supporters via free Quran distributions and raising funds to sponsor suicide attacks in Syria and Iraq by raising money.

• OdaTV released a video allegedly showing ISIS militants riding a bus in Istanbul.

Turkish Forces Are Fighting Alongside ISIS

• On October 7, 2014, IBDA-C, a militant Islamic organization in Turkey, pledged support to ISIS. A Turkish friend who is a commander in ISIS suggests that Turkey is "involved in all of this" and that "10,000 ISIS members will come to Turkey." A Huda-Par member at the meeting claims that officials criticize ISIS but in fact sympathize with the group (Huda-Par, the "Free Cause Party", is a Kurdish Sunni fundamentalist political party). BBP member claims that National Action Party (MHP) officials are close to embracing ISIS. In the meeting, it is asserted that ISIS militants come to Turkey frequently to rest, as though they are taking a break from military service. They claim that Turkey will experience an Islamic revolution, and Turks should be ready for jihad. (See HERE and HERE.)

• Seymour Hersh maintains in the London Review of Books that ISIS conducted sarin attacks in Syria, and that Turkey was informed. "For months there had been acute concern among senior military leaders and the intelligence community about the role in the war of Syria's neighbors, especially Turkey. Prime Minister Recep Erdogan was known to be supporting the al-Nusra Front, a jihadist faction among the rebel opposition, as well as other Islamist rebel groups. 'We knew there were some in the Turkish government,' a former senior US intelligence official, who has access to current intelligence, told me, 'who believed they could get Assad's nuts in a vice by dabbling with a sarin attack inside Syria - and forcing Obama to make good on his red line threat."

• On September 20, 2014, Demir Celik, a Member of Parliament with the people's democratic party (HDP) claimed that Turkish Special Forces fight with ISIS.

Turkey Helped ISIS in Battle for Kobani

• Anwar Moslem, Mayor of Kobani, said on September 19, 2014: "Based on the intelligence we got two days before the breakout of the current war, trains full of forces and ammunition, which were passing by north of Kobane, had an-hour-and-ten-to-twenty-minute-long stops in these villages: Salib Qaran, Gire Sor, Moshrefat Ezzo. There are evidences, witnesses, and videos about this. Why is ISIS strong only in Kobane's east? Why is it not strong either in its south or west? Since these trains stopped in villages located in the east of Kobane, we guess they had brought ammunition and additional force for the ISIS." In the second article on September 30, 2014, a CHP delegation visited Kobani, where locals claimed that everything from the clothes ISIS militants wear to their guns comes from Turkey. (See HERE and HERE.)

• Released by Nuhaber, a video shows Turkish military convoys carrying tanks and ammunition moving freely under ISIS flags in the Cerablus region and Karkamis border crossing (September 25, 2014). There are writings in Turkish on the trucks.

• Salih Muslim, PYD head, claims that 120 militants crossed into Syria from Turkey between October 20th and 24th, 2014.

• According to an op-ed written by a YPG commander in *The New York Times* on October 29, 2014, Turkey allows ISIS militants and their equipment to pass freely over the border.

• Diken reported, "ISIS fighters crossed the border from Turkey into Syria, over the Turkish train tracks that delineate the border, in full view of Turkish soldiers. They were met there by PYD fighters and stopped."

• A Kurdish commander in Kobani claims that ISIS militants have Turkish entry stamps on their passports.

• Kurds trying to join the battle in Kobani are turned away by Turkish police at the Turkey-Syrian border.

• OdaTV released a photograph of a Turkish soldier befriending ISIS militants.

Turkey and ISIS Share a Worldview

• RT reports on Vice President Joe Biden's remarks detailing Turkish support to ISIS.

• According to the *Hurriyet Daily News* on September 26, 2014, "The feelings of the AKP's heavyweights are not limited to Ankara. I was shocked to hear words of admiration for ISIL from some high-level civil servants even in Şanliurfa. 'They are like us, fighting against seven great powers in the War of Independence,' one said." "Rather than the [Kurdistan Workers' Party] PKK on the other side, I would rather have ISIL as a neighbor," said another."

• Cengiz Candar, a well-respected Turkish journalist, maintained that MIT helped "midwife" the Islamic state in Iraq and Syria, as well as other Jihadi groups.

• An AKP council member posted on his Facebook page: "Thankfully ISIS exists... May you never run out of ammunition..."

• A Turkish Social Security Institution supervisor uses the ISIS logo in internal correspondences.

• Bilal Erdogan and Turkish officials meet alleged ISIS fighters.

Statement for the Record
Submitted by Mr. Connolly of Virginia

On April 16, 2017, the Turkish people will decide whether to expand President Erdogan's powers by rendering the Turkish president the head of state and head of government or to maintain the current parliamentary system with its existing checks and balances. The reform would enable the president to issue decrees, declare emergency rule, appoint cabinet ministers and two-thirds of the country's senior judges without parliamentary approval, and even to dissolve parliament.

This constitutional referendum represents a critical moment for Turkish democracy. Erdogan claims that the proposed presidential system would strengthen Turkey's government in the face of internal and external threats. However, there are widespread concerns about Erdogan's attempts to consolidate power and suppress political dissent, and any discussion of this referendum must consider this context. Formal entrenchment of these administrative powers could accelerate Turkey's slide toward authoritarianism and sound the death knell for its accession to the European Union.

The plebiscite takes place against a backdrop of violence and fear. Last July, disaffected factions of the Turkish military carried out a failed coup attempt that claimed more than 270 lives. Despite a long history of successful and unsuccessful coup attempts in Turkey, there is no doubt that the bombing of the Grand National Assembly building, attempts on the lives of Turkey's civilian and military leadership, and other disturbing images from the night of July 15 inflicted a level of trauma on the Turkish public. A series of terrorist attacks by the Islamic State and the Levant (ISIL) and Kurdish militants have also rattled the Turkish people over the last year and a half.

In the wake of the coup attempt, President Erdogan declared a state of emergency and has subsequently embarked on a sweeping crackdown of dissent. The government has formally arrested more than 40,000 individuals, including 10,000 soldiers. One-third of the general corps for the Turkish military has been dismissed and more than 170 media outlets shut down. The government has suspended or terminated 125,000 private and public sector workers, half of which come from the field of education.

Ostensibly, the target of much of this activity by law enforcement has been the followers of the U.S.-based cleric Fetullah Gulen. More than a dozen universities and 1,000 secondary schools connected to Mr. Gulen have been shuttered, and the government has filed a formal extradition request with the United States. However, many accuse Erdogan of using the coup attempt as an opportunity to quash any and all political opposition or threats to his power. The government has also jailed 13 members of the pro-Kurdish democratic opposition in parliament on terrorism charges, and suspended or incarcerated elected mayors of 82 municipalities in the Kurdish southeast region.

The United States should care about the health of Turkish democracy. As a close ally and one of 28 democracies that comprise NATO, Turkey has been a strategic partner in our capability to respond to regional crises. The United States has a national security interest in ensuring the stability of our ally during this difficult time. That includes reinforcing democratic institutions and helping Turkey hold accountable those responsible for the coup attempt and continued threats to security. However, we must lend this assistance on our terms. The United States will not play handmaiden to a crackdown on dissent that violates our support for democratic principles and engages in human rights abuses.

Turkey's future has to be with the European Union, and the European Union's future must include Turkey. The timing of this constitutional referendum, amidst a sweeping crackdown of free expression and political space for opposition, could magnify concerns about the health of Turkish democracy. I look forward to hearing from our witnesses on how the United States should engage our ally Turkey during this critical test for its democratic future.

Note: Material submitted for the record by the Honorable Dana Rohrabacher, a Representative in Congress from the State of California, and chairman, Subcommittee on Europe, Eurasia, and Emerging Threats, entitled "Islamic State Networks in Turkey," by Merve Tahiroglu and Jonathan Schanzer, Foundation for Defense of Democracies, is not reprinted here but may be found on the Internet at: http://docs.house.gov/Committee/Calendar/ByEvent.aspx?EventID=105842